MARKETING IN YOUR UNDERWEAR:

Stripping Down to the Basics of Sales and Persuasion

By

Connie Ragen Green

Marketing in Your Underwear: Stripping Down to the Basics of Sales and Persuasion

Connie Ragen Green

ISBN Paperback: 978-1-937988-65-4

ISBN eBook: 978-1-937988-66-1

ISBN Hardcover: 978-1-937988-67-8

Hunter's Moon Publishing

https://HuntersMoonPublishing.com

Hunter's Moon Publishing - Connie Ragen Green

P.O. Box 3295

Santa Barbara, CA 93130-3295

Connect with Connie Ragen Green at ConnieRagenGreen.com

Limits of Liability and Disclaimer of Warranty

Warning - Disclaimer

CONNIE RAGEN GREEN'S TITLES

- ☞ *In Pursuit of Healthy-Ness: How I Reinvented My Life with Intermittent Fasting*
- ☞ *Speakers! The Quick Public Speaking to Business Method™ - Turning Your Talk into an Ongoing Revenue Stream*
- ☞ *The Road Trip: An Entrepreneur's Journey of Self-Discovery*
- ☞ *Authors! The Quick Book to Business Method™ - Turning Your Book into an Ongoing Revenue Stream with Ellen Finkelstein*
- ☞ *Doing What It Takes: The Online Entrepreneur's Playbook*
- ☞ *Kids and Money – Teaching Financial Responsibility and Values to Children*
- ☞ *Rethinking the Work Ethic: Embrace the Struggle and Exceed Your Own Potential*
- ☞ *The Transformational Entrepreneur: Creating a Life of Dedication and Service*
- ☞ *Book. Blog. Broadcast. The Trifecta of Entrepreneurial Success*
- ☞ *Write. Publish. Prosper. How to Write Prolifically, Publish Globally, and Prosper Eternally*
- ☞ *Living the Internet Lifestyle: Quit Your Job, Become an Entrepreneur, and Live Your Ideal Life*
- ☞ *The Inner Game of Internet Marketing – with Geoff Hoff*
- ☞ *The Weekend Marketer: Say Goodbye to the '9 to 5', Build an Online Business, and Live the Life You Love*
- ☞ *Time Management Strategies for Entrepreneurs: How to Manage Your Time to Increase Your Bottom Line – with Geoff Hoff*
- ☞ *Huge Profits with a Tiny List: 50 Ways to Use Relationship Marketing to Increase Your Bottom Line*
- ☞ *Essays at the Intersection of Hope and Synchronicity*

- ☞ *Self-Directed: Inspire, Motivate, and Empower Yourself to the Greatness That Lies Within*

... and too many more to mention!

DEDICATION

I dedicate this book to the marketers who inspired me to first pursue, and then continue my journey as a writer, entrepreneur, and marketer in the online space. This includes Marlon Sanders, Joe Vitale, Ellen Finkelstein, Craig Perrine, Ali Brown, Dr. Jeanette Cates, Carl Galletti, Denise Wakeman, Migúel A. de Jesus, and many more thought leaders and geniuses who continue to inspire me each day. These people continue to move me closer to the lifestyle by design I am so blessed to have created for myself, and in an ongoing and ever-changing way.

Without their wisdom and guidance in the form of online and in-person training, courses, books, and conversations over the years, I would still be floundering in my business, or doing something completely different with my life, and that would be a shame for so many reasons.

And I could never leave out the late Cory Rudl, the original pioneer in the online space, whose eBook and audios gave me the courage and inspiration to seek out this world for myself, and to Derek Gehl, who took over for Cory after we lost him right as I was getting started with the basics of an online business in June of 2005. I am forever indebted to these brilliant leaders and innovators who changed the way we use the internet and think about being in business for ourselves.

I also dedicate what I'm sharing here to the newer people who've come online with a dream and a vision as to what this life will hold for them and who will add to the conversation. I too was one of them not so very long ago and am honored to pay it forward each day.

Here's to everyone who has set their sights on having a business that is joyous and profitable, and is ready to market in their underwear by stripping down to the basics of sales and persuasion to achieve all of their goals and dreams!

profits. While we're here together this week, I'll introduce you to two strategies that will free up your time and make this business a scalable one."

For a moment, I thought this was simple marketing on her part, and that she might be getting ready to sell them something that would solve all their issues. But almost immediately I realized that Connie thinks at least two steps ahead of the words she speaks and that she will always figure out the shortest path to solving a problem in a business.

We finished our meal, walked out to the end of the pier, and as we made our way up State Street to go back to the hotel, I overheard the husband whisper to his wife, "I think this trip has already more than paid for itself."

Two more people arrived the next morning, and I watched with awe and wonder as Connie, a self-proclaimed introvert, interacted with the five of us throughout each day.

I had been brought in as an expert with online marketing and copywriting, and Connie deferred to me regularly to share my thoughts and solutions to the questions at hand. Not many people in her position would be as gracious and generous, I'll tell you.

If you have the chance to work closely with Connie in some capacity, take it without hesitation. Whatever you wish to achieve with your business, she'll help you map out a path that will make sense for you.

~ Marcus Demetrius, author, creator, and innovator at
Demetrius International in Cabo San Lucas, Mexico.

PREFACE

As I was making the drive to pick up a friend from a medical appointment this past year, three thoughts popped up in my mind, as simultaneously as humanly possible within a single thought sequence and without crashing into something while going sixty miles an hour along the freeway.

The first was that I had not yet written a book exclusively about marketing, though that is what I've become most known for since coming online as an entrepreneur in 2006.

Secondly, I thought about what marketing means to me on a personal level. I've read close to a hundred books on this topic and by people considered to be legends in this field. Yet, I haven't before shared how these authors and concepts have changed and impacted my life.

More people have told me they wanted me to write a book about marketing than one on any other topic for years. Why haven't I listened until now? I have no good answer to this and not even a mediocre one.

Thirdly, I have sought out and then stepped away from formal training on the topics of business, economics, and marketing on more than one occasion, and there are excellent reasons for this. Again, I haven't shared much about these experiences at all, until now.

While I was a graduate student at San Francisco State University, the marketing they were focused on was related to the corporate world. I had been accepted into their MBA program and was entertaining thoughts of working at one of the corporations in downtown San Francisco after graduation.

I'd made some friends at school, and one day they suggested we take the BART - the Bay Area Rapid Transit – train into the city and have lunch at one of the corporations that opened its cafeteria to the public one day each week. We commenced to do this once a week, and each time at a different location. It only took about a month for me to realize something that I hadn't thought of previously: The only part of the corporate world I liked was eating lunch in their cafeteria. The thought of then returning to a cubicle, or even to a corner office with a view, held no appeal and was of no interest to me whatsoever.

I completed the first year of the MBA program and then returned to southern California that summer.

As a side note, I took one creative writing course each semester I was attending San Francisco State, and the Dean of their College of Creative Arts at that time was August Coppola, so my future as a writer was now firmly entrenched in my brain. There are no coincidences and this was most certainly serendipitous.

Coppola had also designed the Tactile Dome at the Exploratorium in San Francisco over a decade earlier. This became a joyous place to visit on the weekends as I was finding and defining myself and my future. But the world of academia continued to beckon to me.

Most recently, I applied to and was provisionally accepted to a doctoral program in Economics at the University of California at Santa Barbara. Ultimately, I did not clear my provisions and went in person to speak with the Department Chair to explain why my application should be withdrawn and the spot opened up to someone on the waiting list.

All of these experiences lead us back to the book you have in front of you, and one that I hope will whet your whistle in terms of studying marketing as something important to all of us in one way or another.

Why am I publishing this information now? I'm ready to pull back the curtain, and the growing multitude of people who follow me are ready as well to receive what I am openly sharing. If you've been stymied as to how to become a marketer in your own right, you're in the right place at the right time to learn what you need and know that much of what I'm sharing is already intuitive and part of your thinking, whether or not you realize it at this moment.

Contents

PROLOGUE

STARDATE:316697.3217275495

In my dream, I'm sitting behind an oversized, solid oak desk and gazing over the top of my computer at the room around me. I am aware of my two little dogs playing at my feet and the sunlight is coming in through the Plantation shutters, casting a shadow at an angle across the desk. The view is of palm trees and mountains in the near distance and it's still and quiet.

As I strain to hear the sounds coming from somewhere downstairs, I hear Coldplay singing "Fix You" and I pause to listen to the lyrics...

"*When you try your best, but you don't succeed*

When you get what you want, but not what you need

When you feel so tired, but you can't sleep

Stuck in reverse"

My thoughts come rushing in like the tide during a full moon, enveloping me in the soft, transparent swash while emitting a tingling sound that seems to come from somewhere far away in the universe.

I'm not sure if I am still asleep or if I am now awake, in that hazy space that exists somewhere between fantasy and reality. Will everything I'm describing here come true, is it already true, or is it the fantasy of someone steeped in doubt and uncertainty?

I had been stuck in reverse after the unexpected death of my closest childhood friend, Tory. He had choked on food and passed away several months earlier, on the day before Christmas in 2005 and I wasn't even attempting to accept what had happened and move past the experience.

I had wanted him to be there to experience and share in the success I was already having with my new online business. We had so many plans for the future, yet he had skipped ahead and departed the planet early, leaving me behind to figure everything out on my own.

Initially, I had felt betrayed and questioned the life experience and purpose for myself and everyone who graces our planet with their presence. Over the previous months, I had come to realize that much of what I had believed to be true, in terms of how my life would unfold as I grew older and, hopefully, wiser was not based in truth at all, but instead intertwined with fear. I had a lot of inner work to do.

I was seeking happiness, but not of the garden variety. No, I had no interest in pursuing anything commonplace as a part of my life experience ever again. And, it was not hedonistic happiness that had caught my fancy either.

Pursuing pleasure as an antidote to experiencing pain seemed much too shallow for what I had in mind.

I wanted it all, so I committed to the pursuit of eudaimonic happiness, where authenticity and virtue would lead to life purpose and personal growth. This approach is also the more sustainable one, fostering a long-term view where taking responsibility is the norm and preferring a sense of meaning and a moral compass take precedence over immediate gratification and selfishness.

If you had told me in 2006 that I was on my way to becoming a marketing strategist, bestselling author of more than twenty-five bestselling books, and a sought-after mentor to people all over the world seeking both financial and time freedom to live life on their terms as I and many others were doing, I would have thought I was still inside of a dream instead of wide awake and living my dreams out loud and in person.

Come along with me and I'll share the secrets of the Universe, at least the ones that will convince you that marketing rules the world. And by the way, the dream I described above *did* become my reality, right down to the Plantation shutters, as soon as I visualized it in my mind's eye as my reality. Now that, my friend is some powerful marketing, with some sales and persuasion tossed in for good measure.

SECTION ONE

WHAT IS MARKETING?

"Few things have filled me with such breathless awe as flying in the black of night across oceans and continents and looking out my window upon the infinite glory of millions of stars."

~ Dieter F. Uchtdorf

Marketing is the one topic that remains elusive yet desirable to those who venture into the waters of sales, persuasion, authorship, and authority. It's about so much more than making money by convincing someone to buy something. To even think of it in this way is to defy gravity and believe the Sun rising each day is simply an accident of chance.

To some, there is nothing more shameful and embarrassing than being thought of as a marketer. Yet to others, myself included, marketing is the secret sauce of a successful business endeavor and even life itself.

We'll begin with a textbook definition, sanitized and rewritten in a way that has removed at least some of the bias, stereotype, and insanity that has become too commonplace during the almost twenty years since I first began my purposeful study of and personal practice in this area.

We'll begin with a broader definition of marketing, then hone it down to something more manageable and reflective of what you need in your business.

Marketing refers to activities a company undertakes to promote the buying or selling of a product or service. Marketing includes advertising, selling, and delivering products to consumers or other businesses.

It is also the process of exploring, creating, and delivering value to meet the needs of a target market in terms of goods and services; potentially including the selection of a target audience; selection of certain attributes or themes to emphasize in advertising; operation of advertising campaigns; attendance at trade shows and public events; design of products and packaging attractive to buyers; defining the terms of sale, such as price, discounts, warranty, and return policy; product placement in media or with people believed to influence the buying habits of others; agreements with retailers, wholesale distributors, or resellers; and attempts to create awareness of, loyalty to, and positive feelings about a brand.

Marketing is most often done by the seller, typically a retailer or manufacturer. Sometimes tasks are contracted out to a dedicated marketing firm or advertising agency.

As you can see, this subject is about much more than can be described with any single definition or explanation.

So, let's talk about marketing in the context I am sharing with you here: It's a way to share what you are creating, as well as the products, courses, programs, and resources created by others as a way to earn income with an online business.

Is this something people can do from home... Perhaps in their underwear instead of dressing up and going into an office? I'm so glad you asked! This is exactly what this book is about and there's no time like the present for us to get started.

Your adventure awaits, so let's begin!

Chapter 1

Marketing Makes the World Go 'Round

Jerusalem bells a-ringin', Roman Cavalry choirs a-singin'.Be my mirror, my sword, my shield, missionaries in a foreign field. For some reason, I can't explain, I know Saint Peter won't call my name. Never an honest word, but that was when I ruled the world.

~ Viva la Vida, Chris Martin, et al.

Everyone wants to rule the world, or at least that's what I've heard. I wondered: Could marketing be the way to rule at least my little corner of the planet? I had to find out and was finally ready to do the work, the deep work few will explore to discover and claim as their own.

I have to admit that I never gave any thought to marketing until I was in college. As a sophomore at UCLA, I took a course in economics and was introduced to a whole new world that went beyond academics and reason. It was as though I became entrenched in a parallel universe each time I stepped through the classroom door. We met in Haines Hall, one of the four original buildings built in 1927, along with Royce, Powell, and Kinsey Halls that surrounded the quadrangular courtyard known as "the quad." It was 1973 and I was about to expand my thinking in previously – at least to me – unimaginable ways.

Although I can still picture the professor in my mind, I can no longer remember his name. He had long blonde hair and wore raggedy blue jeans – before those became trendy - and sandals with no socks. In my mind, I had labeled him as a hippie, but this wasn't a negative or derogatory thought on my part, just a way of thinking of him and giving him space in my mind.

We learned about microeconomics - which focuses on the study of individual markets, sectors, or industries, and macroeconomics – the branch of economics that deals with the performance, structure, behavior, and decision-making of an economy as a whole. It wasn't boring for me, but then I didn't expect this class and topic to be anything exciting.

I can remember one day while I was having lunch in the quad's outdoor garden with two of my classmates from this class, we began sharing our thoughts on economics and the power of what we were being taught. One person said, "I feel like I can rule the world with what we're learning here. But in a positive way, of course."

I did not have a comment to add to that conversation. I still felt like economics was a dry subject that I would mostly forget about once the class was over. But that all changed and I perked up my ears when the professor began teaching us about the stock market. I will never be an expert in this area, nor is it my intention to become one on any level. However, learning about commodities and how the markets fluctuate depending on many factors was interesting to me.

While many of my fellow students chose to invest, and then subsequently lose money by playing the stock market while we were in class together that quarter, I chose to focus on the academics of the subject and approach it from a different perspective. They were using scholarship awards and student loans to fund their habit, and while not illegal at that time, it was certainly frowned upon.

Instead, I followed the commodities and during the following decade did well with coffee and banana futures. It was a tiny article in the Los Angeles Times one day, reporting incidences of flooding throughout South America that caught my attention.

When prices began to increase significantly several months later, my investments skyrocketed and people close to me thought I had a future in working towards a career in the stock market. However, I quickly decided it wasn't for me and continued to focus on completing my coursework for my intended goal. I earned my degree with a dual major in political science and psychobiology and went on to attend Law School in New York City.

But we're getting off-topic here. What does economics have to do with marketing?

The Connection Between Marketing and Economics

Marketing is so many things rolled into one and will be defined by people in various ways, depending upon their beliefs, values, and experiences, as well as by the item being marketed to them or by them at any given moment.

In my thinking, marketing is selling, persuading, convincing, explaining, demonstrating, branding, positioning, informing, educating, sharing, and entertaining.

There are also multiple uses for marketing, and some of these may surprise you.

During the two decades I was active in real estate, both as a broker and a residential appraiser, I thought I was marketing the properties I was involved with, as well as the services I provided to my clients.

It turned out that the most important thing I was marketing was myself. That's right, once I learned how to introduce myself to my clients and to gain their trust with everything I said and did, my income increased.

Before I had learned anything at all about persuasion and studied the great work of marketing experts like Robert Cialdini, Joe Vitale, and Marlon Sanders, I came to understand the importance of letting others discover the skills and knowledge I possessed.

This led to my becoming an expert witness in cases where a real estate transaction had become a legal case.

One time, I was asked to be an expert witness by an attorney representing a couple who had purchased a home soon after I had appraised it.

The foundation of the home had cracked, causing irreparable damage. As I took the witness stand, I thought back to the day when I had driven to the neighborhood and slowly noted each home within a two-block radius in terms of style, appearance, age, condition, and more.

It's kind of funny... I just realized that while I'm writing this book I'm going back and forth with my marketing. As I write something here, it gives me an idea for something I'm marketing to my online community. This includes my own products, courses, and services, as well as those from people I know and act as an affiliate for with their products.

Economics and marketing are closely related fields that intersect in several ways. Both disciplines are concerned with understanding and influencing consumer behavior, albeit from different perspectives and with different goals. Here are some key connections between economics and marketing:

The "Human Behavior" Connection

Economics and marketing both study how people make choices and decisions. Economics focuses on the rational aspects of consumer behavior, such as utility maximization and decision-making based on preferences and constraints.

Marketing, on the other hand, delves into the psychological and emotional aspects of consumer behavior, including the role of branding, advertising, and consumer perceptions.

Pricing Strategies and Economics

Economics provides the theoretical foundation for pricing strategies. Concepts like supply and demand, elasticity, and price discrimination are central to understanding how prices are set.

Marketers use these economic principles to optimize pricing strategies that align with the organization's goals and market conditions. This alone is a reason why everyone building a business must make a focused study of marketing and the related topics I'm discussing within these pages.

The Importance of Market Research

Both economics and marketing heavily rely on data analysis and market research. Economists often use data to analyze trends and market dynamics, while marketers use market research to understand consumer preferences, segment markets, and develop products or services that meet customer needs.

Competition and Market Structure

Economics examines market structures, including perfect competition, monopoly, oligopoly, and monopolistic competition. Marketers take these concepts into account when strategizing, and understanding how market structures affect pricing, competition, and the development of marketing tactics.

Advertising and Information Science

Economics explores the role of information in markets, known as "information economics." Marketers leverage this knowledge to create advertising and communication strategies that inform and persuade consumers. The concept of asymmetric information, where one party has more information than another, is particularly relevant to marketing.

The Subfield of Behavioral Economics

Behavioral economics is a subfield that blends insights from both economics and psychology. It looks at how people often deviate from purely rational decision-making and instead make choices influenced by cognitive biases and heuristics. Marketers use insights from behavioral economics to design persuasive marketing campaigns and nudge consumers toward certain decisions.

Resource Allocation

Both economics and marketing are concerned with the allocation of resources. Economics deals with resource allocation on a macroeconomic scale, while marketing focuses on allocating resources within an organization to maximize market share and profitability.

Analyzing Market Demand and Supply

Economics analyzes market demand and supply, helping marketers understand how changes in these factors can impact the overall success of their products or services. Market demand reflects consumer preferences, while market supply relates to a company's production capabilities.

Government Regulations with Economics and Marketing

Economics and marketing intersect in the context of government regulations, particularly in areas like antitrust laws, consumer protection, and advertising standards. Economists may study the economic impact of regulations, while marketers must navigate the legal landscape and ensure compliance.

You can see that economics and marketing share a common interest in consumer behavior, pricing, competition, and resource allocation. While economics provides the theoretical framework, marketing applies these principles to create strategies that promote products and services, ultimately affecting consumer choices and market outcomes. The synergy between these two fields is essential for businesses to succeed in a competitive market environment.

But how do economic factors like employment statistics, inflation, confidence and stability in government, pandemics, and military involvement and participation in worldwide conflicts affect the marketing of products and services to the marketplace?

Economic factors such as employment statistics, inflation, confidence and stability in government, pandemics, and military involvement and participation in worldwide conflicts have a significant impact on the marketing of products and services to the marketplace.

These factors can influence consumer behavior, market conditions, and marketing strategies in various ways:

Consumer Purchasing Power and Employment

- ☞ High employment rates typically lead to greater consumer confidence and increased purchasing power. Marketers can target consumers with disposable income for higher-end products and services.
- ☞ Inflation erodes the purchasing power of consumers. Marketers may need to adjust pricing strategies to account for rising costs and ensure products remain affordable.

Consumer Confidence and Trust

- ☞ Confidence and Stability in Government: Political stability and a well-functioning government can foster consumer confidence and trust in the marketplace. Marketers can leverage this trust to build brand loyalty and make long-term investments.
- ☞ During pandemics, trust in businesses' commitment to safety and public health becomes essential. Marketers must emphasize safety measures and transparent communication to maintain consumer trust.

Market Demand and Consumer Behavior

- ☞ Consumer behavior can change drastically during pandemics, leading to increased demand for certain products (e.g., healthcare items) and decreased demand for others (e.g., travel and hospitality). Marketers need to adapt quickly to shifting consumer needs and preferences.

Military Involvement and Worldwide Conflicts

These events can lead to uncertainty and anxiety, impacting consumer behavior. Consumers may become more cautious about spending, which can affect the marketing of non-essential goods and services.

Economic Factors as Market Opportunities: Economic fluctuations can create opportunities for marketers. For example, during a recession, budget-friendly products and services might gain more traction, while marketing messages focused on cost savings can be effective.

In times of economic uncertainty, marketers may need to adjust their marketing mix, such as offering discounts or promotions to entice cost-conscious consumers.

Supply Chain and Production Costs

Rising inflation and economic instability can lead to increased production costs. Marketers may need to rethink their pricing strategies or explore cost-cutting measures.

A stable government can create a more predictable regulatory environment for businesses. Marketers can operate with confidence and make long-term plans.

During military conflicts and pandemic events, emergency regulations or restrictions may apply. Marketers must stay informed about any relevant regulations and adapt their strategies accordingly.

International Markets and Global Economic Factors

For companies operating in international markets, economic conditions in different countries can vary significantly. Marketing strategies must consider the economic factors specific to each market.

Communication and Messaging

During pandemics or times of military conflict, marketing messages should be sensitive to the prevailing conditions. Companies may need to adjust advertising and messaging to reflect the current climate and consumer sentiment.

Economic factors play a crucial role in shaping marketing strategies and consumer behavior. Marketers must be agile and responsive, adapting their approaches to economic conditions, consumer sentiment, and regulatory changes to succeed in a dynamic marketplace. Understanding the interplay between economic factors and marketing is essential for businesses to effectively reach their target audiences and achieve their goals.

Guerilla Marketing

Guerilla marketing is a way to drive publicity and, as a result, brand awareness by promoting using unconventional methods designed to evoke surprise, wonder, or shock.

This style of marketing is the creative use of novel or unconventional methods to boost sales or attract interest in a brand or business. These methods are often low- or no-cost and involve the widespread use of more personal interactions or with viral social media messaging.

This marketing method has increased in popularity with the rise of ubiquitous mobile and connected technologies that can amplify messaging and focus on target groups of consumers.

Some consumers may be more attracted by guerrilla marketing campaigns as they may be more interesting and daring, while others may be turned off because of the perceived "disruptive" aspects of this style of marketing.

Marketing in the Online Space

While I'm sharing strategies and concepts that have worked extremely well for me since I started my business in 2006, I want to make it clear that most of what I do is online.

Yes, I have also spent years as a consultant and strategist with companies, corporations, service businesses, and professionals who run their businesses primarily with a brick-and-mortar, physical location, and I've written a bestselling book to help people with their brick-and-mortar businesses titled *Local Business Marketing: Making the Phone Ring for Businesses Everywhere.*

This book has become a training guide for those who wish to be directly involved in the marketing of their businesses or even to create a lucrative business or side hustle by working closely with small business owners. This is an excellent way to get started as a marketer, and many times the businesses are across the country or even in another country, instead of being located in your city or community.

But the focus of what I'm sharing here with you is intended to be for people who already have, or want to create a business that can be run exclusively on the internet.

Chapter 2

Everyone's a Salesman

"The best marketing strategy ever: CARE."

~ Gary Vaynerchuk

My mother walked me to school and back each day during my years in elementary school. She didn't drive and we never had a car, so this was a normal and natural part of my upbringing. As to why she didn't drive, that's simple: My mom never encountered anyone who knew how to sell her on the idea.

Once or twice a week on our way to school, we would cross the street at the traffic signal and visit the corner store. This was so I could buy something with the change I had saved up from my allowance and from doing odd jobs for friends and neighbors.

Mr. Roth ran the corner store. He was a heavyset man who was always wearing a sweater, even when the weather did not call for it. He also wore a smile that turned his face into a welcome sign for all who entered.

On one of these occasions, Mr. Roth put down his broom – he swept up every bit of dust that entered the store from the busy street – and motioned for me to follow him down the aisle where he kept the candy. He knew I had a sweet tooth and encouraged it in a kindly manner that was irresistible.

He pointed out that he was now carrying some new candy bars that I might not be familiar with, and my mouth watered as he held up each one, just out of my reach, and described the taste and the texture in great detail.

He then asked me a question I did not know the answer to, but I was sure he would tell me after I thought about it for a minute or two.

"Do you ever bring candy to school to share with your friends? I mean, to sell to them because they do not get to stop by here themselves?"

I understood fully well what he meant. I was the only student who walked to school instead of arriving by car each day. Everyone, including the other kids already knew that, and seldom did anyone even ask me about it.

However, what I did not understand and could not answer was his question about selling candy to my classmates. Was that even allowed? Would anyone want to buy candy? Why would I do this?

Mr. Roth gave me a minute to think before jumping in with his thoughts on the matter he was proposing.

"Connie, you know that I purchase the candy and everything else I carry in the store from companies that are called distributors. I buy at the wholesale price and sell to my customers at the retail price. The difference between wholesale and retail is my profit."

I nodded. This I understood, at least as much as a 4th grader can grasp such a concept.

He continued.

"What I am proposing here is that you could buy a few candy bars to the price I pay for them – the wholesale price – and then sell to your friends at the retail price... plus a premium for your time and efforts.

"But I don't understand why the kids wouldn't just buy the candy they wanted at the store, instead of having to pay me extra money to get it."

"Because someone is driving them to school, and that person does not want to make a stop on the way there or back. You have what they want, and they have the money to pay a little extra."

When Mr. Roth said it like that, I got it! We completed our transaction, with me taking five candy bars from him "on consignment" and my mother and I were out the door and on our way to school. Now, I just had to figure out how to let everyone know I had candy for sale, and in a way that would encourage them to buy some from me.

I thought of making a sign, but that would be too obvious and would've been tantamount to standing in the middle of the schoolyard, holding up a candy bar, and not saying a single word. No one would understand what I was doing, the action I wanted them to take, and why.

The missing link in my plan was a clear and simple marketing strategy. As we walked the final block to my school, I began to visualize exactly what I could do that would work.

Playing it cool as I hugged my mother and watched her walk away, I sauntered through the gate and into the school with an air of confidence that wasn't typical for me. Today was the beginning of something special and my demeanor was meeting the moment.

I stopped at the drinking fountain and took a long, deep breath before pulling my hair back with one hand and turning on the water with the other.

Most of the students had already arrived. They were gathered in clusters on the playground, laughing and making small talk while waiting for the bell to ring. Some of the boys were chasing each other and a few were practicing for the high jump in a far corner of the yard.

As I scanned the area to find the perfect spot, I began to see my classmates in a different light. Although I couldn't have verbalized it back then, I was now seeing them as prospects and potential customers instead of simply the kids I was going to school with that year.

I needed a spot where I could attract some attention without making a scene. I also needed some customers who would most likely be willing to buy from me. Shading my eyes from the sun with my left hand while thrusting my right hand into my purse to take out some inventory, I held my head high and walked over to where Randy Tepper and Loren Grayson were in a huddle with their heads together.

"Hi, guys. What's up?" I could hear myself talking and I sounded completely normal.

"Hey." Randy was a minimalist when it came to speaking to girls.

I held up two Fifth Avenue bars and smiled.

"Wanna buy some candy?"

What happened next was life-changing.

"Sure. How much?" It was Loren, his eyes fixed on the candy bars I was holding.

"Um, do you just want one or both of them?"

There was what I was perceiving as an awkward pause, so I had to think quickly. Let's see, these sold for ten cents each, I had agreed to pay Mr. Roth fifteen cents for two, and I wanted to make some profit.

"They're twenty-five cents each, but I could give you both for forty cents."

Loren answered before I could add anything, making this process a smooth one, like taking candy from a baby, but in reverse and to a 4th grader who was most definitely not a baby.

"Keep the change, Connie. Thanks!"

He had thrust two quarters into my left hand and gently taken the two bars from my right. I nodded and a smile formed on my lips. Inside, I was jumping up and down.

Phyllis was next, and she approached me without my saying a word. She bought one and then motioned for Belinda to come over.

The first bell rang, and I was left with just one candy bar I decided to save for myself. By the time the second bell had rung and we were lined up and ready to follow our respective teachers into our classrooms, I already had several orders for what they wanted me to bring the next day.

Although I had sold Girl Scout cookies for a month before quitting the Brownies a year earlier, on this day I finally joined the ranks of being a full-fledged salesperson and an entrepreneur.

My mother didn't mention anything about it on the walk home because she'd more than likely forgotten about the morning's activities at Mr. Roth's store. This gave me the time to play it over and over in my mind, from the moment we'd entered the store until I had sold the next to last candy bar just before the bell had rung.

I had learned and internalized a few things. First, I needed people who were likely to purchase what I had for sale. These were my prospects who would become customers the moment they purchased from me. Then, I needed to get those people directly in front of me so they'd know what was for sale. This was my traffic. The playground in the morning at school was perfect, at least to begin with. Finally, I needed to present the items for sale in a way that made sense and was convincing. This was my offer.

In the online space, this configuration translates to a list, traffic, and an offer. It's all you need to officially be in business. Yes, marketing and sales are simple concepts to understand and implement. Keeping it simple and consistent is the true test of our skills.

Here, I had people I knew who were interested in having candy to eat when it was not available from any other source in that time and space. While they were all gathered together on the playground, I was able to attract attention to myself. My offer was an excellent one.

Another thing I thought about that day was how I was able to make a convincing argument as to why they should pay me almost double the price for something they could get for less if only they could find a way to make that happen.

Within a week or so, three different boys had begun bringing candy and other items to sell in the yard in the morning and also at lunch and after school. But they didn't do very well and finally, the teachers got wind of our operations and shut us down for good.

Again, I used the experience as a learning opportunity. What had they done differently than me? Why didn't they sell much? What had made my approach successful, while theirs fell flat?

While everyone is a salesman, not all salespeople make sales. If you find that you get a lump in your throat or a knot in your stomach when you think about selling, the best way to get past this thinking is to make it a habit each day.

Make an offer to a friend or family member. It doesn't even have to involve an exchange of money, as bartering for products and services is an excellent model I've used many times. Remain relational instead of transactional and you be on your way to mastering the sales process.

Chapter 3

The Debut of the Marketing Madwoman

"Conversations with customers will increase sales, even if the product or service is never mentioned."

~ **George Farris**

The first time someone referred to me as the "Marketing Madwoman" I have to admit I was somewhat taken aback. What did they mean exactly? How was I expected to respond? Did it mean mad like I was angry about something or mad like I had lost my mind? *Was* it a compliment, or were people poking fun at me? I would soon find out.

It was the fall of 2008 and I was in Austin, Texas to attend a marketing conference hosted by people I knew well, and on the topics of traffic and conversion.

I was in the elevator with my friend and Mastermind partner, Dr. Jeanette Cates. She lived in Austin and I had flown in a day early to take in the sights and spend additional time with her.

She had taken me downtown to the Congress Avenue bridge to see the bats, and to a restaurant that sat directly on the shore of Lady Bird Lake.

The elevator stopped on the street level of the hotel and a man stepped inside. Jeanette recognized him and introduced me. I can remember his deep hazel eyes smiling at me as she told him that I was someone he should get to know. She explained that I had become a "super affiliate" and was on my way to becoming the next "Marketing Madwoman."

As the elevator came to a stop on the top floor, the man took my hand in his and squeezed it gently, as if to etch this memory into both of our minds. We all exited the elevator and went our separate ways, but my only thoughts were to find out who the previous marketing madwoman was and where she was these days. I continue to wear this moniker with pride. And by the way, the man in the elevator with Jeanette and I that day was Dan Kennedy, one of the great marketers and innovators of all time and whom I am now honored to call my friend.

Your Marketing is a Part of Everything You Do

No matter what the situation, I have learned how to make my marketing a part of everything I say and do. Bringing your words and actions back to some aspect and perspective of your business is the way to build a lucrative and profitable lifestyle.

Here are a few examples...

If I'm out and about with people I know, I look for a reason – okay, an excuse – to share a relevant story with them. The conversation inevitably leads back to my business and I'm able to explain what I do in different ways to practice getting my message out to the world.

If I'm waiting in line at the post office or even in the waiting area for a medical appointment, I'll strike up a conversation with a stranger and look for a way to redirect the small talk toward my business. It's so much fun and I make a game out of it.

You never know who you might meet in this way, and one day while waiting in line at the post office I had a conversation with author and entrepreneur Barbara Winter that led to a years-long friendship until she passed away in 2022.

My primary discussions around business focus on sales, persuasion, and marketing...

- ☞ In my email messages
- ☞ My blog posts
- ☞ Personal interactions
- ☞ And in my books...

Remember, you're looking for the pain point to draw the reader or listener in closer to resonate with your message.

I use something called "Before, after, AFTER" which works quite well.

Before: I was working 60 to 70 hours each week as a classroom teacher and in real estate as a listing broker and residential appraiser. I was exhausted and my health was already beginning to suffer. I wondered if having enough money to own – or at least to be in the process of purchasing - my own home and to help my elderly mother was worth the toll it was taking on me. I didn't know another way to earn as much income as I could with teaching and real estate, which amounted to $125 - $150 thousand a year during the early 2000s.

After: I discovered that people were setting up little businesses on the internet to sell digital information products, courses, services, and eBooks and I decided I wanted to do the same, at least as a side hustle to begin with. I made small amounts of money recommending other people's products, courses, and services through affiliate links and this encouraged me to learn more and take this new business venture more seriously.

AFTER: I achieved my initial goal of replacing my previous income with an online business, and expanded it to include public speaking, authorship, mentoring, and consulting.

Finding My Voice as an Online Marketer

Most of us are not born with the confidence it takes to become a leader in a specific field. Luckily, this makes the world of business a level playing ground for everyone, newbies and seasoned marketers alike.

I knew less than nothing as a beginner in late 2005 and into 2006. When someone first mentioned the concept of having a "voice" when it came to what you were doing in your business, I was intrigued. It turned out that all of us have something of a creative genius potential inside of us already. Allowing this genius to poke its head out and join the world is something else altogether.

An excellent idea for you to find your voice as a marketer is to remember when you made your voice heard at an earlier time in your life. I went back to my childhood first, then to the various jobs I had taken over the decades, and finally to the twenty years during which I was working as a classroom teacher.

My mother and I struggled as I was growing up. There was never enough money and she refused to ask for help. This all came to a head when I was in the third grade.

At that point, I had figured out that people were willing to buy things they wanted and liked, as long as they had enough disposable income to do so. My mother was an artist, and while we were at the beach on the weekends, she and I would collect a few seashells to take home. One day she painted a flower on one of the seashells and I put it in my pocket and took it to school with me the following day.

At recess, I took it out and admired it in the sunlight. A few of the girls came over to see what I had and I told them the story of going to the beach, picking up the seashells, and my mother painting on them.

They were mesmerized by my story and wanted to know if there were more. I was honest and told them this one was the only one I had, but that it was for sale.

I hesitated. Was this a good idea or not? Three of the girls said they wanted to buy it before I even told them the price. I told Jacqueline she could buy it because she had asked me first. I gave them a price of twenty-five cents and promised to have more by the end of the week. As Jacqueline placed the shiny quarter in my hand and held the seashell up to the sunlight, I knew my life had changed forever.

Why did I choose the price of a quarter? Because that was the cost of a hot lunch at school. That day I didn't say I wasn't hungry to avoid the embarrassment of not having any money or any food of my own. That day I had meatloaf and mashed potatoes with gravy, along with a carton of milk and a chocolate cookie baked by the lady who ran the cafeteria. That day, everything changed. Now, I only had to convince my mother to paint more seashells so I could sell them at school.

In an earlier chapter, I shared the story of how I sold candy at school on the playground. Evidently, my voice was so small and scared it took me a year to sell anything to anyone again.

The next time I found my voice was years later when I was first teaching 5th and 6th graders.

Finding My Voice as a School Teacher

There was a shortage of teachers at all grade levels in Los Angeles during the 1980s, so when I began the credentialing program, I was encouraged by my professors to apply for an "emergency credential" downtown at the offices of the Los Angeles Unified School District. I did that in the spring of 1986 in hopes of getting an assignment not too far from home. They informed me that it was up to me to contact the schools and let them know I was available.

I began substituting at several schools and one in particular felt like a good fit for me. By the end of June, I had subbed more than fifty days in almost a dozen schools, including a long-term four-week position in a third-grade classroom where the teacher had come down with chicken pox.

The summer arrived and everyone I knew asked me where I was going to work in the fall. My answer was that I knew one of the schools I had substituted at would contact me when they knew they had an opening. I enjoyed my eight weeks off by swimming, hiking, and camping for two weeks in Yosemite. Sure enough, by the middle of August the school that had been my favorite asked me to begin the year with a long-term position. I wouldn't have a contract but they said that was definitely possible before the end of December.

That weekend was a busy one as I prepared for my first day as a "real" teacher. On Monday morning I was at school bright and early. The teacher's parking lot was right behind Room 3 and I had chosen the spot where I would park each day. As I exited my car and popped the trunk to take out my rolling cart I was startled when two people came up behind me.

It was the Cooks; the couple my new teacher friends had told me about. I turned around quickly to greet them.

"I'm Lillian, and this is Ed," the woman said. She was tall and blonde and dressed like she was going somewhere more formal than the classroom.

Ed extended his hand and I shook it firmly. He hadn't let go when he said, "I'm out in Room 28, in the Gifted Magnet. Do let me know if you need anything."

The two of them gave me the creeps and I now wished no one had told me anything about them. I would be interacting more with Lillian than with her husband, as the regular school didn't mingle much with the Magnet. I knew little about how everything worked on that first day.

My first week was busy and filled with activities and learning for me as well as my students. Whereas I thought I would be using my Spanish in the classroom it turned out that most of the kids had just recently immigrated to the United States.

I discovered that only five of my thirty-eight students were Spanish speaking, and one of them had set a goal of only speaking English at school. More than a dozen of the remaining thirty-five kids spoke some dialect of Latvian, Romanian, Lithuanian, Ukrainian, Farsi, Russian, Polish, Armenian, or Farsi. Two students, a girl and a boy who were first cousins spoke both Hebrew and English but were not allowed to speak English at home.

The remainder of my class was made up of kids from South Central Los Angeles who were being bused in, by choice so they could attend our school.

I was overjoyed at my status as a new teacher and it showed in my energy and enthusiasm. During recess one day the principal called me into his office to let me know that the teacher for whom I was working had called from Sebastopol, a small town in northern California where she wished to relocate to tell him that she had an impending teaching position there. I was so excited and glad I had not spent my summer worrying. Everything was working out and I was on my way.

By Friday I had learned so much and truly connected with my class. For the first time that week I left school soon after dismissal and went straight home to begin planning for the following week. I was filled with hopes and dreams for what my students and I could accomplish during our school year together.

What goes up must come down. It's a universal law of physics and gravity. On Monday morning I would learn that this law applied to feelings of exhilaration as well. On the way in from the parking lot the Cooks approached me and I slowed down to speak with them. Ed locked eyes with me before Lillian began to speak. She explained, in a sugary sweet voice I had not heard out of her during the previous week that they would be resuming their Friday movies this week. I must have had a puzzled look on my face because they both took a step closer to me and she began to explain in greater detail.

"Connie, you're new so I don't expect you to understand. Last school year, the 5th and 6th-grade teachers decided to implement a movie day each week as a way to reward the students who work hard. Ed stops by Blockbuster on Thursday evening and chooses something most everyone will like." I could see Ed nodding out of the corner of my eye and she continued.

"It's a very special day for them, Connie. Sometimes we have popcorn and we turn the lights off so it's almost like being at the movies."

"But what do the teachers do while the movie is playing?" My degree of naïvety at that point in my teaching career was greater than I care to remember all these years later.

"That's the best part, Connie. The teachers – there are four of us, including you, of course – take turns staying with the kids. The others go back to their classroom and get work done. I've promised my husband I won't be bringing any work home again this year and I always keep my promises!"

With this, she threw her head back and laughed so big I could see a crown that was slightly discolored in the back of her mouth. They were both smiling widely and laughing like they had just robbed a bank and gotten away with the perfect crime. I was sickened at what I was hearing and not sure how to react.

"What about the kids who didn't work hard? Where do they go while the movie is on?"

"They come to my room and sit at a table in the back." It was Ed talking now. "They know better than to give me any trouble."

I nodded and we all walked to our classrooms. My smile was pasted on as I greeted teachers, parents, and students. This new predicament made me nauseous and gave me a headache. I went through the motions until recess and then I put my head down on my desk to clear my head and gather my thoughts.

The other teachers involved, including two that I had met before school began while we were setting up our classrooms all had teaching credentials. My credential was for emergency purposes only and would only be cleared after I had taught for two full years and completed my coursework at the university. And this would only occur if I received satisfactory recommendations from my administrators two years in a row.

I wanted to talk to the principal about this. I wanted to say no. I wanted to scream and yell and fight for my kids. But I was too weak to do so and kept my mouth shut. On Friday I sent one of my girls to Mr. Cook's room with the homework she hadn't finished. The rest of my class went to the movies.

We walked together to the room where the VCR and television had been set up and I sat down with them for the first ten minutes or so to see what watching a movie at school would be like. The box the video had come in was on the desk and I picked it up to read more details. The film had been released two years earlier with a rating of PG (Parental Guidance) and the reason for this was stated as "language, innuendo, and potentially scary scenes and situations."

I didn't have any work I needed to finish at school and when I returned to my classroom I sat down in a student's chair and looked up at the front of the room to see it from their perspective.

Was I being too protective? Who was I to go against what a group of veteran teachers had agreed to a year earlier? Perhaps spending a couple of hours each week watching a movie with your friends and classmates was a valuable use of this time.

No, it wasn't! I stood up and felt more strongly than ever that this was a bad idea on many levels. What could I do to bow out of this situation gracefully? The bell rang for our recess and I met my students coming out of the room.

"Was the movie good?" I asked. "What happens at the end? I can't remember."

"The movie isn't over, Mrs. Green. They choose two helpers each Friday to stop the video every twenty minutes so we can take bathroom breaks and talk. We're having popcorn next week." It was Ari talking. He shared that he had seen this movie twice but liked having a day off with his friends.

Without saying a word, I went looking for Mrs. Cook. There was that toothy grin again, waving at me to come over and join her on a bench while the kids were at recess. I allowed some small talk before I inquired as to the amount of time devoted to the movie every Friday.

She explained, slowly and carefully as if she were talking to a small child, how it worked. The movie was drawn out at least until lunch. After lunch the teachers could do what they liked (as if we couldn't beforehand) but most took their classes out for physical education until the end of the school day. Sometimes the kids even brought their backpacks and other belongings out to the yard with them so they could be dismissed from there more quickly when the bell rang.

I thanked her and made an effort to smile. It probably looked like I was trying too hard so I stopped before I walked away. I knew the weekend was going to be a tough one for me. This situation was going to ruin my days off but it had to be this way. On Saturday and Sunday, I transformed into the person I had always wanted to be but hadn't had the intestinal fortitude to manifest. It would be the beginning of the rest of my life and I was ready to move forward.

The week unfolded as it had the previous week, with math and social studies, language arts, science, and more. No one said a word about a movie for Friday and I let it ride. It wasn't until right before recess on Thursday that I brought it up. I asked everyone to close their books and to look up at me because I had something important to discuss with them.

My young charges were so good. They quietly put their things away and folded their hands in front of them. It brought me close to tears to see how they looked to me for guidance and direction. I blinked back the tears and stayed strong. They needed me to be a leader and an advocate for them right now.

Our class discussion was amazing. I asked them if there was anyone who felt like they didn't get to see enough movies at home or the movie theaters. We talked about the movie shown the previous Friday and some of them told me their parents would not let them see it because they were too young. They were honest and open and engaged as we continued.

Then I began drawing on the whiteboard. I explained that I already knew everything I would be teaching them during that school year. They smiled and nodded and someone said that was why I was the teacher and not one of them. Then I made a math problem on the board where I showed the result of me not teaching them for one full day every week throughout the year. We were at school for 36 weeks or 180 days. Twenty percent of that came out to 36 days or just over seven weeks that I would not be teaching and they would not be learning if we had a movie day every week.

"Because I already know all of what I will be teaching you, and I am not thinking about going on to middle school very soon, it honestly feels like I'm stealing from you. And then there's the other part."

They wanted to know what I meant by "the other part."

"I get paid to be your teacher. It's my job, right? And do you know who pays me?"

They guessed the government, the school district, the principal, and even the President of the United States until I told them the answer.

"You pay me. When you buy something at the store and pay taxes, that's part of how it works. When adults pay income taxes and state taxes, that goes towards my paycheck. So, if I feel like I am stealing from you when I only teach you four days a week instead of five, can you imagine how I'll feel if they pay me for five days and I only work for four? That's stealing money from you and your family and all the people who pay taxes who don't even have kids in school. I don't want to steal from anyone."

Then I put it to a vote. I prefaced the voting by saying that if there was anyone who wanted to see the movie for any reason, I would be glad to try to negotiate that on their behalf and would not hold it against them. The result was unanimous. Everyone in my class voted to learn five days a week. And I promised to be the best teacher they would ever remember and make it fun as well. The recess bell rang and then I let some tears flow.

It would be nice if this were the end of the story. During recess word got out to all of the classes involved and those teachers were not happy about what I had done. As soon as my class was settled in and ready for social studies there was a loud banging on our door. I opened it up to find Mrs. Cook glaring at me. I stepped outside into the hallway and she lit into me. Instead of closing the door so we could talk privately I swung the door wide open so my students could hear every word.

She yelled, she cursed, she called me every name in the book. She had worked herself up into a frenzy to the point that she was spraying spittle on my cheek. But I didn't flinch. When she finally quieted down and took a breath the only thing I said was, "It's over. We already voted."

Then I went back inside, closed the door, and picked up the teacher's edition of the social studies book. Then Gregor raised his hand. I called on him and he stood up to get everyone's attention.

"Why didn't you hit her, Mrs. Green?"

Before I could answer Anca stood up and addressed everyone.

"Because if she did that, then we would have a new teacher tomorrow."

I nodded but did not smile. "That is correct. We do not grow as human beings by fighting. We do what is right and help all of humanity by using our words and taking actions that prove we believe in what we say."

I still don't know where those words came from, as they did not feel like my own as I heard them coming out of my mouth. They were inspired and I was prompted to speak them aloud. On that day, I found my voice and the seed was planted that would germinate and grow into something very powerful for my future.

We worked through a lesson in social studies and in that short time they understood that education was about so much more than just reading and answering questions out of a textbook. I was so very proud of them, on that day and forever after.

The Cooks stopped speaking to me after that day, as did at least half a dozen other teachers. A new principal was assigned to our school in January and he soon put an end to movies during school time, unless they were educational in nature and tied to the curriculum.

I stepped up my efforts as a teacher in a variety of ways, including writing, applying for and receiving technology grants, starting a science fair at our school that would now include both the "regular" school students and the gifted magnet for the first time ever, and teaching "bank account" math to the parents who were interested after school. On the rare occasion when I would go into the teacher's lounge at recess or lunch one of the Cooks would inevitably say,

"You'll learn."

This was meant to let me know I was doing too much for the students. They even told me it was making them look bad if I did too much.

My response was always the same...

"And when I do, I'll increase my efforts even further."

You may see a direct correlation between my experiences fighting for the rights of those without a voice, and what we do online by sharing only the most wonderful people, products, courses, and more with our prospects and clients. It's being in service to others is a way that makes a difference for everyone involved. If this makes me a madwoman with my marketing, I'll gladly wear that moniker with a badge of honor.

SECTION TWO

WHY IS MARKETING IMPORTANT?

"Marketing is about values. It's a complicated and noisy world, and we're not going to get a chance to get people to remember much about us. No company is. So we have to be really clear about what we want them to know about us."

~ Steve Jobs

The importance of marketing cannot be overstated. Whether you're a child or an adult, sales and marketing come into play with almost every situation we encounter.

Kids vie for the attention of grownups by marketing themselves as someone who deserves attention and to be heard.

Adults eagerly await the opportunity to be asked "What do you do?" so they may market their skills, experiences, and personality to those who may be interested.

In this section, we'll explore why marketing is important and how to use your skills to improve and change your life.

When we meet someone new and they ask "What do you do?" they have allowed us to market ourselves to them.

We respond according to our perception of what they would be most interested in knowing about us and what we most want them to know about us.

If I'm at a gathering and mingle among a hundred people or more, I'm likely to describe what I do in a dozen different ways.

I'm an author, publisher, entrepreneur, marketer, blogger, writer, marketing strategist, consultant, solopreneur, and online business owner.

Subconsciously, I'm determining how I could serve them, how they could help me, and where this relationship might go.

In my previous life as a classroom teacher and real estate broker and residential appraiser, I did not think in this way.

I was typically introduced to someone as a teacher. They would sometimes ask me what grade level I taught and at which school, but that was usually the end of the discussion.

Seldom did real estate work its way into the conversation. It was only after I had left teaching and real estate during 2006, to come online as an entrepreneur and marketer, that I learned the value of allowing others to view us in more of a three-dimensional manner.

You are doing this to both inform and potentially serve the other person, and this is at the core of what marketing is all about. I would also share a story about my experiences with teaching and/or real estate, as storytelling will always serve to make us more memorable.

My favorite stories include one about selling a home to a teacher at my school, only to discover on the day we were to close and while doing the final walk-through that they would be living across the street from one of the largest gathering places of the Hell's Angels motorcycle groups in the Los Angeles area. While I was sure these buyers would use this as a reason to back out of the deal, it turned out they had already become acquainted with some of their neighbors during the weeks leading up to the purchase of the home and had determined them to be fine neighbors.

There are multiple marketing stories here, including the ones shared by these colorful neighbors with people new to the neighborhood so they would not be judged on misconceptions. Yes, marketing is also extremely important as a life skill.

Pattern Interrupts in Marketing

This is as good a place as any to interrupt what I was thinking about something called pattern interrupts. I recommend you use these when your sales are down, your marketing efforts seem commonplace, and when your sales copy isn't getting the results you want, or perhaps not at all.

Pattern interrupts are a concept commonly used in marketing to capture attention and break the typical flow of thought or behavior. The idea is to disrupt the expected sequence of events or thoughts, causing individuals to pay closer attention to what's being presented. In marketing, pattern interrupts can take various forms:

Using unexpected or attention-grabbing visuals in advertisements or presentations can disrupt the viewer's thought pattern. This might include bright colors, unusual imagery, or unexpected movements.

Introducing unexpected or unconventional messaging can jolt the audience out of their automatic thought processes. This could involve posing a thought-provoking question, making a surprising statement, or using humor in unexpected ways.

Interactive content such as quizzes, polls, or surveys can interrupt the passive consumption of information and engage the audience directly, encouraging them to participate and become more invested in the content.

Altering the pace of communication can also serve as a pattern interrupt. For example, starting with a slow and deliberate presentation and then suddenly speeding up can capture attention.

Narratives that start unexpectedly or unconventionally can create a pattern interrupt. This might involve beginning a story with an unexpected event or turning point to pique curiosity and draw the audience in. Storytelling is perhaps my favorite of all pattern interrupts.

Offering unexpected incentives or promotions can interrupt the typical consumer decision-making process and encourage immediate action. Limited-time offers or exclusive deals can create a sense of urgency that prompts people to act. I did this most recently with an affiliate promotion, where all of the other affiliates had email lists and followings much larger than my own. By offering what I labeled as "Special Bonuses" I was able to win the contest that was set up. I only do this when I know the product creators personally and have the greatest respect for them, as well as for the product or course they are offering.

Highlighting a stark contrast between the current situation and a desired outcome can interrupt habitual thinking patterns and motivate action. This might involve emphasizing pain points or illustrating the benefits of a product or service in a compelling way.

Pattern interrupts are effective because they disrupt the brain's tendency to filter out familiar or routine stimuli, causing individuals to pause and pay attention to something that stands out. By leveraging pattern interrupts strategically, marketers can increase engagement, drive conversions, and ultimately achieve their marketing objectives.

The Power of Storytelling: Using Narrative as a Pattern Interrupt in Marketing

In today's fast-paced world, capturing and retaining the attention of consumers has become increasingly challenging for marketers. With an abundance of information constantly vying for their attention, individuals have developed a remarkable ability to filter out traditional advertising messages. In this landscape, marketers are turning to innovative techniques to break through the noise and engage their target audience. One such technique that has proven to be highly effective is the use of storytelling as a pattern interrupt in marketing.

Storytelling is an age-old art form that has the unique ability to captivate and resonate with people on a deep and emotional level. By harnessing the power of narrative, marketers can create compelling experiences that not only capture attention but also leave a lasting impression on consumers. In the context of marketing a product or service, storytelling serves as a potent pattern interrupt, disrupting the typical consumer mindset and inviting individuals to become active participants in the brand's narrative.

So, how exactly does storytelling function as a pattern interrupt in marketing? Let's delve deeper into the mechanisms at play:

At its core, storytelling is about creating intrigue and capturing attention. By weaving a narrative that is both compelling and relevant to the target audience, marketers can immediately grab the viewer's attention and draw them into the story. This initial engagement serves as a crucial pattern interrupt, breaking through the monotony of traditional advertising and sparking curiosity in the consumer's mind.

One of the most powerful aspects of storytelling is its ability to evoke emotions. Whether it's joy, sadness, excitement, or empathy, a well-crafted story has the potential to elicit a wide range of emotions in the audience. By tapping into these emotions, marketers can forge a deeper connection with consumers, transcending the transactional nature of traditional advertising. This emotional resonance serves as a potent pattern interrupt, compelling individuals to pay closer attention to the brand's message.

In a crowded marketplace, differentiation is key to standing out from the competition. Storytelling offers a unique opportunity for brands to differentiate themselves by communicating their values, mission, and personality memorably. By sharing authentic and compelling stories, marketers can carve out a distinct identity for their brand, making it more memorable and relatable to consumers. This differentiation serves as a powerful pattern interrupt, disrupting the consumer's perception of the brand and setting it apart from competitors.

In today's digital age, consumers are bombarded with an overwhelming amount of content on a daily basis. As a result, their attention spans have become increasingly fragmented, making it challenging for marketers to hold their interest. Storytelling addresses this challenge by creating an immersive experience that keeps consumers engaged from start to finish. By crafting narratives that unfold over time and leave room for exploration and discovery, marketers can prolong the consumer's engagement with the brand, increasing the likelihood of conversion and retention.

Ultimately, the goal of any marketing campaign is to inspire action – whether it's making a purchase, signing up for a newsletter, or sharing content with friends. Storytelling has a unique ability to motivate action by appealing to the consumer's emotions, values, and aspirations. By aligning the brand's message with the consumer's own narrative, marketers can empower individuals to take meaningful action that aligns with their desires and goals. This call to action serves as a final pattern interrupt, prompting consumers to move beyond passive engagement and take concrete steps towards engaging with the brand.

Storytelling represents a powerful tool for marketers seeking to break through the clutter and capture the attention of their target audience. By leveraging the innate power of narrative, brands can create compelling experiences that disrupt the typical consumer mindset and foster deeper engagement and connection. Whether it's through captivating visuals, relatable characters, or compelling story arcs, storytelling has the potential to transform marketing campaigns from forgettable to unforgettable. So, the next time you're looking to market a product or service, consider the power of storytelling as a pattern interrupt – you might just find yourself creating a story worth sharing.

Chapter 4

The Importance of Copywriting in Marketing with Carl Galletti

"Most people bury the most important stuff deep in their sales copy. Your audience is too busy to try to guess what your point is, so if you take too long to tell them, they won't be there to find out."

~ Carl Galletti

I asked my friend, mentor, and colleague, professional copywriter and marketing legend Carl Galletti to share his experiences and expertise in the area of copywriting with you here. My recommendation is that you linger over this chapter, making notes, stopping to think along the way, and internalizing what is being shared with you here so that you may begin to incorporate these concepts and strategies into your business over time.

Legendary copywriter Carl Galletti is widely regarded as one of the most successful and influential copywriters in the direct response marketing industry. He has written numerous successful direct mail packages and sales letters that have generated millions of dollars in sales for his clients.

Copywriting in Marketing

Firstly, it's important to realize that every business is a marketing business because everyone has to sell something and marketing is the mechanism to do that.

Copywriting is the art and science of communicating the marketing message through language. Both marketing and copywriting come under the umbrella of advertising, both free and paid.

Copywriting plays a crucial role in marketing and is integral to the success of any marketing campaign. Its importance can be highlighted through several key aspects:

1. Communicating Value

Copywriting articulates the value proposition of a product or service. It translates features and specifications into benefits and advantages that matter to the customer, making the value they offer clear and compelling.

2. Engaging the Audience

Effective copywriting captures the attention of the target audience. It speaks in a language that resonates with them, addressing their needs, desires, and pain points, which helps in building a connection and engaging them on a deeper level.

3. Driving Conversions

The ultimate goal of most marketing efforts is to drive actions, whether it's making a purchase, signing up for a newsletter, or downloading a guide. Copywriting is designed to persuade and motivate the audience to take these actions, effectively converting interest into action.

4. Building Brand Identity

Copywriting contributes significantly to the voice and personality of a brand. Consistent use of tone, style, and language in copy helps in building a recognizable brand identity, which can distinguish a brand in a crowded marketplace and foster brand loyalty among consumers.

5. SEO and Online Visibility

In digital marketing, copywriting is essential for search engine optimization (SEO). Well-crafted copy that incorporates targeted keywords can improve a website's ranking on search engine results pages (SERPs), increasing visibility and driving organic traffic to the site.

6. Educating the Audience

Good copy doesn't just sell; it also informs and educates. By providing valuable information and insights, copywriting helps consumers make informed decisions about their purchases, establishing trust and credibility for the brand.

7. Supporting Multiple Channels

Copywriting is versatile and supports various marketing channels, including email marketing, social media, websites, and advertising. Each channel requires a nuanced approach to copywriting to effectively communicate and engage with the audience through that medium.

8. Emotional Connection

Copywriting often leverages emotional triggers to create a stronger bond between the brand and its customers. By appealing to emotions such as happiness, fear, excitement, or trust, copywriting can influence purchasing behavior and brand perception.

9. Competitive Advantage

Innovative and compelling copy can provide a competitive advantage. It differentiates products and services in a way that technical specifications or features alone cannot, highlighting unique selling points and creating a preference for the brand.

10. Measurable Results

Copywriting's impact on marketing campaigns can be directly measured through metrics such as conversion rates, click-through rates, engagement rates, and more. This data-driven approach allows for optimization and improvement, making copywriting an essential tool for achieving marketing objectives.

Copywriting is foundational to marketing success. It not only helps in effectively communicating the value of products or services but also plays a pivotal role in engaging customers, driving conversions, and building a strong brand identity.

What is Advertising?

In the early 1900's in Chicago, there was an advertising agency by the name of Lord & Thomas. It was one of the major ad agencies of the day, chiefly due to a junior partner named Albert D. Lasker.

Although Lasker was the driving force behind the agency, he didn't have a good definition of advertising and felt that this was holding the agency back from being even more successful.

Enter an ex-Canadian Mountie turned ad man named John E. Kennedy.

Kennedy defined advertising for Lasker as:

"Salesmanship in Print."

The concept of "Salesmanship-in-Print" is a fundamental principle in copywriting and marketing. This concept underscores the idea that effective copywriting should mimic the persuasive, engaging, and informative qualities of a skilled salesperson, but in a written format. Here's an exploration of this concept:

Core Principles

1. Persuasion: Just like a good salesperson uses persuasive techniques to convince a customer to make a purchase, effective copywriting persuades the reader through the power of words. It involves crafting messages that appeal to the readers' emotions, desires, needs, and pain points, encouraging them to take a specific action, such as buying a product or signing up for a service.
2. Engagement: Salesmanship-in-print involves engaging the reader from the beginning to the end, much like a salesperson would maintain a customer's interest during a conversation. The copy should be compelling, relatable, and tailored to the target audience, keeping them interested and invested in the message being conveyed.
3. Clarity and Conciseness: A skilled salesperson communicates the benefits of a product or service clearly and succinctly. Similarly, effective copywriting conveys its message clearly, avoiding ambiguity and confusion. It delivers the core message

in an easily digestible format, ensuring that the main points are understood and remembered.

4. Building Trust and Credibility: Just as trust is crucial in the relationship between a salesperson and a customer, salesmanship-in-print aims to build trust between the brand and the reader. This is achieved by providing honest, accurate information, using testimonials or endorsements, and addressing potential objections upfront.
5. Call to Action: Every successful sales interaction ends with a call to action (CTA), encouraging the customer to make a decision. Similarly, effective copy always includes a clear CTA, guiding the reader on what to do next, whether it's making a purchase, learning more about a product, or contacting the company for more information.

Application in Marketing

"Salesmanship-in-Print" is applied across various marketing materials, including but not limited to:

- ☞ **Print Ads:** Where space is limited, and the message needs to be persuasive and to the point.
- ☞ **Landing Pages:** Designed to convert visitors into leads or customers, using persuasive copy that leads to a clear CTA.
- ☞ **Email Marketing:** Where personalized, engaging content drives the recipient towards a specific action.
- ☞ **Social Media:** Crafting messages that stand out in a crowded feed and engage the audience effectively.
- ☞ **Content Marketing:** Through blogs, articles, and guides that inform, educate, and subtly persuade the reader towards a brand's offerings.

In essence, "Salesmanship-in-Print" is about leveraging the written word to replicate the personal, persuasive interaction a salesperson has with a customer, adapted to the context of marketing materials. It's a timeless concept that continues to inform and shape effective copywriting strategies in the digital age, highlighting the importance of persuasive communication in driving marketing success.

Lasker Builds Lord & Thomas into an Icon in Advertising

As soon as Lasker heard the "Salesmanship-in-Print" definition he knew it was the right one. He thereafter used it to skyrocket Lord & Thomas to the #1 ad agency of its time. The agency still exists today under the name Foot, Cone, & Belding; named after the three people Lasker sold the agency to when he retired.

Top advertising, marketing and copywriters have been using that definition ever since. And it is as valid today as it was then.

Of course, when other forms of media like radio and TV came along it was more broadly defined as...

"Salesmanship Multiplied."

When we talk about "Salesmanship Multiplied" versus "Salesmanship-in-Print," you're looking at two sides of the same coin with some nuanced differences. Both concepts revolve around the idea of using persuasive techniques to sell products or services, but they do so in slightly different contexts and scales.

Salesmanship-in-Print

Let's start with "Salesmanship-in-Print." This concept, as you already know, is about translating the skills and techniques of a live salesperson into written form. It's like having a conversation with your audience through an ad, a brochure, or a website, without being there in person.

The aim here is to convince someone to take action, whether it's buying a product, signing up for a newsletter, or just engaging more deeply with a brand. You're using words to create a one-on-one connection, much like a salesperson would do face-to-face, but your audience can be much larger since anyone who reads your copy is effectively being "spoken" to.

Salesmanship Multiplied

Now, think of "Salesmanship Multiplied" as taking that one-on-one conversation and amplifying it across multiple channels and platforms, reaching a vast number of people simultaneously. It's not just about the written word anymore; it's about using every tool in the toolbox—videos, podcasts, social media, email, and more—to replicate that salesmanship at a scale that traditional print methods can't match. The essence of persuasion and engagement is still there, but you're now operating on a much larger stage, with the potential to interact with countless individuals at the same time.

Similarities

Both concepts rely heavily on the fundamentals of good salesmanship: understanding your audience, communicating clearly and persuasively, addressing needs and desires, overcoming objections, and encouraging action. Whether you're crafting a meticulously worded ad (Salesmanship-in-Print) or orchestrating a multi-channel marketing campaign (Salesmanship Multiplied), the goal is to connect with your audience in a meaningful way and convince them to buy what you're selling.

Differences

The primary difference lies in scale and scope. With "Salesmanship-in-Print," your reach is inherently limited by the distribution of the print material. You're engaging in a one-to-many conversation, but the "many" is confined to those who come across the physical or digital copy of your message. "Salesmanship Multiplied," on the other hand, leverages the power of technology and the internet to broadcast your message far and wide, engaging with a potentially global audience across multiple touchpoints.

Furthermore, "Salesmanship Multiplied" allows for a greater degree of interaction and engagement. While "Salesmanship-in-Print" is somewhat static—a printed ad doesn't change once it's out there—"Salesmanship Multiplied" can be dynamic. You can tweak your message based on real-time feedback, engage directly with customers through social media, and use analytics to refine your approach on the fly.

While both "Salesmanship-in-Print" and "Salesmanship Multiplied" are about persuading people to take action, the latter magnifies the principles of salesmanship across a broader spectrum of channels and opportunities. It's like the difference between having a heart-to-heart with someone in a coffee shop and speaking to a packed auditorium with a microphone in your hand—both require skill and authenticity, but the scale and method of delivery are worlds apart.

The trouble, however, with both of these definitions is not with the changing media but with the fact that most people don't understand "Salesmanship" well enough to properly and effectively apply the definition.

Most people think of salesmanship as "coercing someone to buy something against their will."

And, of course, expert sales practitioners know that nothing could be further from the truth. Real salespeople know that salesmanship is the art and science of matching people with a problem for which the product is the solution.

Expert salespeople can do this one-on-one. However, having to sell one on one is only practical for high-ticket products. Lower-priced products need to be sold more efficiently and to a broader audience. And that's where advertising, marketing, and copywriting come into play.

The Two Types of Advertising

What we've discovered is that there are two types of advertising: direct response and institutional.

When you dive into the world of advertising, you'll come across two distinct strategies: "Institutional Advertising" and "Direct Response Advertising." Understanding the difference between these two can significantly impact how you perceive and interact with various marketing efforts.

Institutional Advertising

Think of Institutional Advertising as the long game. This strategy isn't about immediate sales or getting you to take quick action. Instead, it's focused on building a brand's image, reputation, and identity over time. When you see ads that highlight a company's values, community involvement, or its role in sustainability, that's Institutional Advertising at work. The aim here is to shape your perception of the brand, fostering a positive relationship and loyalty without directly urging you to buy a product or service right now.

But without being able to directly measure the results, there is a lot of waste and wrong decisions that are made with this type of advertising.

Direct Response Advertising

On the flip side, Direct Response Advertising is like a sprint. This strategy demands action from you, the viewer, right after you encounter the ad. Whether it's clicking a link, making a phone call, or completing a purchase, the ad's success is measured by how effectively it can convert your interest into a tangible action. These ads are highly targeted, often personalized, and come with a clear call to action (CTA). They're designed to elicit an immediate response, making them highly measurable and often more cost-effective in the short term.

It also tells you directly and immediately whether your approach is effective or not. Most copywriting techniques were and are still based on direct response advertising and copywriting.

Why Direct Response Advertising Can Be Considered Better

Most ad people, especially copywriters, consider Direct Response Advertising/Copywriting as being "better" than Institutional Advertising. The answer lies in its tangibility and accountability.

Measurability: With Direct Response Advertising, you can track results in real time. You see exactly how many people clicked, called, or bought because of an ad. This immediate feedback allows for quick adjustments to maximize effectiveness.

- ☞ Cost-Effectiveness: Because you can measure the impact directly, you can also gauge the return on investment (ROI) more accurately. This helps in optimizing your ad spend, ensuring you're getting the most bang for your buck.
- ☞ Targeting: Direct Response Advertising allows for precise targeting. You can tailor your message to speak directly to a specific audience, increasing the chances of eliciting a response.

This level of specificity is harder to achieve with broad, brand-building campaigns.

- ☞ Urgency: By creating a sense of urgency (e.g., limited-time offer, exclusive deal), Direct Response Advertising can drive quicker conversions. It taps into the human instinct to not want to miss out, pushing you towards taking action.
- ☞ Engagement: This type of advertising fosters a direct line of communication with the audience. It's not just about broadcasting a message; it's about starting a dialogue. Each response is an opportunity to engage further, deepening the relationship between you and the brand.

In essence, Direct Response Advertising is more useful and profitable for sole entrepreneurs and small businesses.

Most advances in advertising, marketing, and copywriting are made through direct response because it reveals the techniques that produce the best results.

Many of the established techniques of copywriting were created in the mail order industry where results were critical to the success of an advertising campaign.

Copywriting Formulas

Let's dive into some of the most effective direct response copywriting formulas, breaking them down into simple, digestible explanations:

1. AIDA: Attention, Interest, Desire, Action

   Attention: Grab the reader's attention with a compelling headline or opening.

   Interest: Keep their interest with fascinating details, benefits, and facts.

   Desire: Build desire for your product or service by highlighting its unique value proposition and how it solves a problem or fulfills a need.

   Action: End with a strong call to action (CTA), urging the reader to take a specific step.

2. PAS: Problem, Agitate, Solution
   - Problem: Start by identifying a problem that your target audience faces.
   - Agitate: Amplify the problem by discussing its consequences and making it feel more immediate and pressing.
   - Solution: Present your product or service as the solution, explaining how it addresses the problem effectively.
3. FAB: Features, Advantages, Benefits
   - Features: List the features of your product or service.
   - Advantages: Explain how these features stand out from the competition.
   - Benefits: Most importantly, show how these features translate into real benefits for the user, focusing on the positive outcomes and emotions they will experience.
4. 4 P's: Picture, Promise, Prove, Push
   - Picture: Paint a vivid picture of the life or situation the reader could have by using your product or service.
   - Promise: Make a promise about the core benefit they will receive.
   - Prove: Back up your promise with evidence, such as testimonials, statistics, or case studies.
   - Push: Encourage the reader to take action with a persuasive CTA.
5. QUEST: Qualify, Understand, Educate, Stimulate, Transition
   - Qualify: Identify the target audience to make sure your message is being read by the right people.
   - Understand: Show empathy and understanding of their needs or problems.
   - Educate: Provide information about how your product or service can solve their problem.
   - Stimulate: Create excitement and desire for your solution.
   - Transition: Lead smoothly into a CTA, making the next step clear and easy.

6. STAR: Situation, Task, Action, Result
    Situation: Describe a scenario or problem that your target audience can relate to.
    Task: Outline the task or challenge that needs to be addressed to solve the situation.
    Action: Detail the action taken, ideally using your product or service.
    Result: Share the successful outcome of taking that action, focusing on the benefits experienced.
7. The Bridge: Before, After, Bridge
    Before: Paint a picture of the problem or situation before your product or service.
    After: Describe the positive scenario after your product or service has been used.
    Bridge: Explain how your product or service acts as a bridge from the 'before' state to the 'after' state.
8. FABB: Feature, Advantage, Benefit, and Benefit of the Benefit
    Feature: This is a factual statement about the product or service, such as what it is or what it does. It's the basic characteristic or function, like "waterproof up to 30 meters."
    Advantage: Here, you explain why the feature is useful. It's about how the feature stands out from competitors or how it can be utilized in a way that adds value, like "allows for underwater photography."
    Benefit: This goes deeper into how the feature and advantage make a difference in the customer's life. It's the answer to "What's in it for me?" For instance, "capture memorable moments while swimming or diving without worrying about water damage."
    Benefit of the benefit: This final step elevates the message by connecting the benefit to a deeper, emotional, or long-term impact. It answers the question of why the benefit matters on a personal or emotional level, like "create lasting memories with loved ones and enjoy

reliving your adventures through high-quality underwater photos."

These formulas are not just techniques but are the foundations of compelling, persuasive copy that connects with readers on a human level. The key is to use these formulas not as strict rules but as guides to help you understand your audience deeply and communicate with them in a way that resonates with their needs and desires. Each formula has its strengths, and the best copywriters skillfully blend elements from multiple formulas to create copy that is not just effective but unforgettable.

Let's take a couple of these formulas and show some detailed examples:

First #2...The PAS (Problem-Agitate-Solution)

This formula is a potent method for crafting messages that resonate deeply with your audience. It's a three-step approach designed to capture attention, stir emotions, and then offer a resolution. Let's break it down:

Problem: Identify a challenge or issue that you know your audience is facing. This step is crucial because it shows that you understand their struggles or needs. It's like saying, "I see what you're going through."

Agitate: Once you've highlighted the problem, you amplify it. This doesn't mean making it worse than it is, but rather, digging into why this problem is particularly bothersome, inconvenient, or painful. It's about poking at the issue to evoke a stronger emotional response, making your audience feel the urgency or discomfort of their situation even more.

Solution: After you've amped up the tension, you present your product or service as the solution to the problem. This is where you show how you can alleviate their pain, solve their problem, or meet their need. It's your moment to shine by saying, "Here's how I can help."

Let's dive into actionable strategies that can elevate your "Marketing in Your Underwear" business. Here's how the PAS (Problem-Agitate-Solution) formula can be applied to craft compelling marketing messages, offering real-world examples tailored to help you thrive.

Example 1: Mastering Social Media with Ease

Problem: Imagine your days consumed by hopping from one social media platform to another, trying to keep your content fresh and engaging. This endless cycle not only saps your energy but also steals time from growing your empire.
Agitate: Every second spent in this social media maze is a missed opportunity to connect with your tribe or to brainstorm your next big product. The frustration builds, knowing your potential is capped by the confines of manual posting.
Solution: Enter our revolutionary social media management tool. Picture yourself dispatching posts across all platforms with a single click from your cozy home office. Suddenly, you're reclaiming hours, focusing on what truly moves the needle - your business growth and genuine customer engagement.

Example 2: Conquering the SEO Battlefield

Problem: Your digital storefront is hidden on the dreaded second page of Google search results, invisible to eager customers searching for exactly what you offer.
Agitate: Each day in this digital obscurity is a blow to potential sales. The world remains unaware of your unique solutions, and with every click on a competitor's link, your opportunity to shine dims further.
Solution: With our bespoke SEO optimization service, we catapult your site into the limelight. Visualize your offerings dominating search results, drawing in a flood of visitors-turned-customers, all while you craft your next big idea in your favorite lounge pants.

Example 3: Crafting Online Courses with Zero Frustration

Problem: The dream of sharing your expertise through an online course is clouded by the daunting tech setup and endless troubleshooting.
Agitate: Time ticks away as your course remains just an idea, not a revenue-generating reality. With each passing day, the gap widens between your current state and where you could be - impacting lives and earning passively.
Solution: Our intuitive online course platform changes the game. Imagine effortlessly bringing your course to life, engaging with students worldwide, all while enjoying the comfort of creating from your couch, coffee in hand.

Example 4: Transforming Emails into Unmissable Events

Problem: Your emails languish in inboxes, overlooked and unopened, rendering your carefully crafted messages ineffective.
Agitate: The disheartening low engagement feels like shouting into the void, wasting precious energy and potential revenue on emails that fail to resonate with your audience.
Solution: Leap into our dynamic email marketing software, where creating irresistible emails becomes second nature. Envision your open rates soaring as each email becomes a must-read for your audience, all achieved in your slippers and tee.

Example 5: Leveraging Time with Virtual Assistance

Problem: Your day-to-day is bogged down with tasks that, while necessary, don't propel your business forward, leaving you little room for strategic growth or personal freedom.
Agitate: The constant juggle is exhausting, a far cry from the entrepreneurial dream you envisioned. You know deep down that your time could be so much more impactful.
Solution: Our virtual assistant services offer a lifeline. Picture delegating these tasks with ease, freeing you to focus on your passions and scale your business, all from the serene comfort of your home office.

"Marketing in Your Underwear" isn't just about working in comfort; it's about finding smart, effective ways to grow your business and connect with your audience on a deeper level. Through these examples, you'll discover how to apply the PAS formula to not only capture attention but to convert that attention into action and loyalty, all while enjoying the freedom and flexibility of running your business your way.

Now, let's dive deeper into copywriting formula #8...

FABB: Feature, Advantage, Benefit, and Benefit of the Benefit:

This is a marketing concept used to effectively communicate the value of a product or service. The idea is to not only describe what a product or service does (Feature) and why it's better than the alternative (Advantage), but also how it positively impacts the customer (Benefit), and then take it a step further by explaining the extended value or impact (Benefit of the Benefit).

The FABB copywriting formula is a powerful approach to crafting compelling marketing messages. Here's an explanation of each component:

Feature: This is a factual statement about the product or service, such as what it is or what it does. It's the basic characteristic or function, like "waterproof up to 30 meters."

Advantage: Here, you explain why the feature is useful. It's about how the feature stands out from competitors or how it can be utilized in a way that adds value, like "allows for underwater photography."

Benefit: This goes deeper into how the feature and advantage make a difference in the customer's life. It's the answer to "What's in it for me?" For instance, "capture memorable moments while swimming or diving without worrying about water damage."

Benefit of the benefit: This final step elevates the message by connecting the benefit to a deeper, emotional, or long-term impact. It answers the question of why the benefit matters on a personal or emotional level, like "create lasting memories with loved ones and enjoy reliving your adventures through high-quality underwater photos."

Here are 5 examples illustrating these concepts:

1. Smart Thermostat
   Feature: Wi-Fi connectivity and mobile app control.
   Advantage: Allows you to adjust your home's temperature from anywhere.
   Benefit: Saves on energy bills by letting you control heating and cooling more efficiently.
   Benefit of the Benefit: The money saved on energy bills can be used for other household needs or savings, contributing to financial well-being.

2. Waterproof Smartwatch
   Feature: Waterproof up to 50 meters.
   Advantage: Can be worn during swimming or in the shower without damage.
   Benefit: Eliminates the need to remove the watch frequently, ensuring continuous health and activity tracking.
   Benefit of the Benefit: Continuous health tracking leads to more accurate health data over time, enabling better personal health insights and improvements.

3. Electric Vehicle (EV)
   Feature: Electric propulsion with a 300-mile range per charge.
   Advantage: Reduces the need for frequent charging and eliminates gasoline consumption.
   Benefit: Saves money on fuel and reduces greenhouse gas emissions.
   Benefit of the Benefit: Contributing to environmental sustainability while also potentially increasing the vehicle's resale value due to its eco-friendly nature.

4. Learning Management System (LMS) with AI Recommendations
   Feature: AI-powered course recommendation engine.
   Advantage: Personalizes learning paths based on the user's progress, strengths, and weaknesses.

Benefit: Makes learning more efficient and effective, helping users achieve their goals faster.

Benefit of the Benefit: Faster achievement of learning goals can lead to quicker career advancements and personal development, enhancing life satisfaction.

5. High-Fiber Breakfast Cereal

   Feature: Contains 10 grams of fiber per serving.

   Advantage: Helps promote better digestive health compared to lower-fiber options.

   Benefit: Contributes to a feeling of fullness, which can help in weight management.

   Benefit of the Benefit: Effective weight management can lead to improved overall health, including reduced risk of chronic diseases and enhanced quality of life.

These examples show how articulating the feature, advantage, benefit, and the extended benefit can more deeply connect with customers by clearly outlining not just the immediate value, but also the long-term impact of a product or service.

Copywriting

Although it would be impossible to adequately cover the subject of copywriting in the limited space available here, the above is a good head start. And let's just extend that a bit with the six most important points to keep in mind. For more on copywriting, visit: ScientificAdvertising.com

Headlines

David Ogilvy once said: "The headline is the most important element in most advertisements. It is the telegram which decides the reader whether to read the copy."

> *"On average, five times as many people read the headline as read the body copy. When you have written your headline, you have spent eighty cents out of your dollar."*

David Ogilvy's insights into the importance of headlines in advertising remain profoundly relevant, even in today's digital marketing landscape. His comparison of the headline to a "telegram" underscores its role as a decisive factor in capturing the reader's attention and determining whether the body copy will be read at all. This principle, that a headline acts as the gateway to the content, highlights its critical importance in any marketing communication.

The Function of Headlines

The headline's primary function is to grab attention in a sea of information. It must stand out, provoke curiosity, and promise value, compelling the reader to invest time in reading the content that follows. In an era where consumers are bombarded with messages across multiple channels, the headline's role as an attention-grabber cannot be overstated.

The Economics of Headlines

Ogilvy's metaphor, equating the crafting of a headline to spending eighty cents out of a marketing dollar, speaks volumes about its value. This analogy highlights the disproportionate impact of the headline relative to the rest of the content. Given that on average, five times as many people read the headline as the body copy, its ability to effectively communicate the essence and appeal of the advertisement is crucial for engaging the majority of the audience, who may not venture beyond it.

Crafting Effective Headlines

Creating a compelling headline is both an art and a science. It involves understanding human psychology, being concise yet powerful with words, and encapsulating the promise of the underlying content. Here are some key considerations:

- ☞ Clarity: The headline should clearly convey what the reader can expect from the content. Ambiguity may intrigue but can also confuse or mislead, potentially alienating the audience.

- Relevance: It must speak directly to the interests, needs, or desires of the target audience, making an immediate connection that prompts further reading.
- Benefit: Highlighting a clear benefit or value proposition to the reader can make the difference between engagement and indifference.
- Emotion: Headlines that evoke an emotional response, whether it's curiosity, excitement, or even fear, tend to be more effective in driving readership.
- Uniqueness: In a crowded marketplace, a headline that stands out by offering something new, surprising, or counterintuitive can capture attention more effectively.

The Digital Evolution

In the digital age, the principles Ogilvy espoused have only grown in importance. With the advent of search engine optimization (SEO), the role of headlines has expanded beyond just capturing attention to also ensuring discoverability online. The challenge now lies not only in appealing to human readers but also in satisfying the algorithms that determine visibility in search results.

Moreover, the proliferation of social media has amplified the impact of headlines. A compelling headline can significantly increase the likelihood of content being shared, extending its reach and impact far beyond the initial audience.

David Ogilvy's assertion about the paramount importance of headlines in advertising offers timeless wisdom. In the current digital landscape, where content is abundant and attention spans are short, the ability to craft an effective headline is more crucial than ever. It's not just about spending "eighty cents out of your dollar" wisely; it's about making every word count to ensure your message not only reaches but also resonates with your audience. As marketers and content creators, focusing on honing this skill can make the difference between being heard in a noisy world or fading into the background.

Open With Your Big Guns

> *"You cannot bore people into buying your product – you can only interest them in buying it."*
>
> **– David Ogilvy**

Get to your best, most interesting (to the reader) stuff right up front. It is the fuel that carries your reader through the rest of the copy. You DO want them to get to your offer and call-to-action, don't you?

The adage "Open with your big guns" encapsulates a vital principle in marketing and advertising: the importance of capturing your audience's attention from the outset. As suggested by the insight that "You cannot bore people into buying your product – you can only interest them in buying it," the initial moments of interaction between your message and its audience are critical. In these moments, you must spark interest, stir curiosity, and engage the reader's emotions. This approach is not just a tactic; it's a fundamental strategy to ensure your message is heard, understood, and acted upon.

The Importance of a Strong Opening

In the sea of content that floods our daily lives, a strong opening act as a beacon, drawing readers into your narrative. The beginning of your copy should highlight the most compelling aspects of your offering. Whether it's a groundbreaking feature, an unmatched benefit, or an irresistible offer, leading with this information grabs attention and sets the tone for the rest of the communication.

Interest as the Catalyst

Interest is the key that unlocks your audience's attention and willingness to engage further with your message. It transforms passive readers into active participants, eagerly seeking to learn more about what you're offering. This interest, once sparked, is the fuel that propels the reader through the rest of the copy, guiding them towards your ultimate goal: the offer and call-to-action (CTA).

How to Craft a Compelling Opening

Understand Your Audience: Know what resonates with your audience. What are their needs, desires, or problems that your product or service can address? Tailor your opening message to speak directly to these points.

- ☞ Highlight the Benefit: People are interested in how your offering can improve their lives. Start by clearly articulating the most compelling benefit of your product or service.
- ☞ Use Powerful Language: Choose words that evoke emotion, create vivid images, or provoke thought. The right language can make your opening irresistible.
- ☞ Incorporate Storytelling: Humans are naturally drawn to stories. If appropriate, start with a narrative that illustrates the value of your offering in a relatable and engaging way. (For more on storytelling, you can download this excellent document: *Seven Story Secrets That Skyrocket Sales*...by Vin Montello at: ScientificAdvertising.com/vin)
- ☞ Leverage Social Proof: Opening with a testament to your product's effectiveness, such as customer testimonials or endorsements, can quickly build interest and trust.

Keeping the Momentum

Once you've captured the reader's interest with your opening, the challenge is to maintain it. Ensure that the subsequent copy continues to build on the initial promise, providing more details, deepening the emotional connection, and leading smoothly to a clear, compelling CTA. Every piece of information should feel like a natural progression from the intrigue sparked at the beginning.

The Role of the CTA

The CTA is your culmination point, but it's only effective if your audience is engaged enough to get there. A strong, interest-driven opening ensures that your readers stay with you every step of the way, making them more likely to act when they reach your CTA. It's here that the initial investment in a compelling start pays off, converting interest into action.

Opening with your big guns isn't just about making a splash; it's about leveraging the brief window of attention your audience gives you to create a lasting impact. By immediately presenting the most interesting and valuable aspects of your offering, you lay a foundation of interest and engagement that carries the reader through to your desired action. Remember, in the realm of marketing, boredom is the enemy of conversion. Interest, on the other hand, is your most powerful ally.

Make Your Copy Easy to Read and "You" Oriented

Use short words, they're more powerful. Also, short sentences and short paragraphs. One of the most successful copywriters today writes mostly in single-sentence paragraphs.

Speak directly to your audience by using "You" and "Your" (2nd person singular) rather than "We" and "Our." Sometimes you can briefly use "I" and "My" during a credentialling section but you must switch your language as soon as possible to address the reader directly and personally. Otherwise, you risk being "interesting" rather "interested."

Making your copy easy to read and "You" oriented is not just about simplifying the language; it's about creating a direct, intimate connection with your audience. The goal is to make your readers feel like you're speaking to them personally, understanding their needs, desires, and challenges, and offering a solution that speaks directly to their situation. Here's how to refine your approach:

Use Short Words, Sentences, and Paragraphs

Short words are the backbone of powerful, impactful writing. They're easy to understand and pack a punch. Similarly, short sentences and paragraphs keep the reader moving smoothly through your copy, maintaining engagement without overwhelming them with dense blocks of text. This approach is not about dumbing down content but making it accessible and enjoyable to read. A modern trend among successful copywriters is the use of one-sentence paragraphs. This technique adds rhythm and emphasis, making key points stand out and resonate with the reader.

The Importance of Word Choice

Mark Twain famously highlighted the importance of choosing the right word, noting the vast difference between "lightning" and "lightning bug." This analogy underscores the power of precision in language. The right word can evoke strong emotions, create vivid images, and drive the reader to action, while the wrong word can confuse, distract, or even alienate your audience. Every word should serve a purpose, contributing to the overall message and emotional impact of your copy.

Speak Directly to Your Audience

Personalizing your copy by using "You" and "Your" is a proven strategy to increase engagement. This second-person singular approach makes your message feel like a one-on-one conversation, directly addressing the reader's interests and needs. It's about making them the focus of your message, not your company or product. While "We" and "Our" can occasionally be used to build credibility or share your brand's story, the primary focus should always return to "You" and "Your" to maintain that personal connection.

Credentialing with "I" and "My"

There are moments, particularly when establishing credibility or sharing personal anecdotes, where "I" and "My" can be briefly introduced. This humanizes the message and can help build trust. However, it's crucial to pivot back to focusing on the reader as quickly as possible. The aim is to demonstrate how your experience or expertise benefits them, shifting the spotlight back to addressing their needs and how they stand to gain.

Interested vs. Interesting

Your copy should aim to be interested in your readers, not just interesting to them. This subtle shift in focus means you're prioritizing their needs, desires, and how they can benefit from what you're offering.

Being "interested" involves addressing their experiences and pain points, and providing solutions that resonate on a personal level. It's a more engaging and empathetic approach that fosters a stronger connection and encourages action.

Crafting easy-to-read, "You" oriented copy is an art that balances simplicity with engagement. By employing short, impactful words, sentences, and paragraphs, and speaking directly to your reader, you create a compelling narrative that resonates on a personal level.

Remember, the essence of effective copywriting lies in being genuinely interested in your audience's well-being, guiding them toward realizing how your offer enriches their lives. Through careful word choice and a focus on the reader, your copy can become a powerful tool in converting interest into action.

The Big Idea

"You will never win fame and fortune unless you invent big ideas."

– David Ogilvy

The concept of "The Big Idea" as heralded by David Ogilvy, one of the founding fathers of advertising, underscores the transformative power of groundbreaking and innovative ideas in the realm of marketing and beyond. Ogilvy's assertion that fame and fortune are the rewards of those who invent big ideas speaks to the core of what drives progress in any field, particularly in the competitive and ever-evolving landscape of marketing.

The Essence of the Big Idea

A Big Idea is not just any idea. It's a concept that breaks through the clutter of everyday messages, capturing the imagination of the audience and leaving a lasting impact. It's innovative, bold, and immediately recognizable, carrying with it the power to change perceptions, influence behavior, and even alter market dynamics. The Big Idea is at the heart of campaigns that resonate on a deep level with consumers, becoming part of the cultural fabric and often outliving the products or campaigns that spawned them.

Why Big Ideas Matter

In a world inundated with information and choices, the Big Idea serves as a beacon that draws attention and fosters engagement. It differentiates brands in a saturated market, providing a clear and compelling reason to choose one product over another. Big Ideas have the power to:

- Elevate Brands: They lift a brand from the realm of the ordinary, imbuing it with meaning and purpose that resonate with consumers.
- Drive Innovation: Pursuit of the Big Idea pushes boundaries and challenges the status quo, leading to innovation in products, services, and marketing strategies.
- Create Legacy: Many brands are remembered not just for their products but for the Big Ideas they introduced, which often become benchmarks in advertising history.

Crafting the Big Idea

Finding your Big Idea requires a deep understanding of your audience, a willingness to take risks, and the creativity to see beyond the conventional. Here's how to cultivate the soil from which Big Ideas can grow:

- Immerse Yourself in Insights: Understand your audience's desires, fears, and aspirations. Big Ideas often come from a profound insight into what moves and motivates people.
- Foster Creativity: Create an environment where creativity thrives, where ideas are welcomed, and failure is seen as a step towards success.
- Be Bold: Don't shy away from ideas that seem too ambitious or out of the ordinary. The Big Idea often lies beyond the boundaries of comfort and convention.
- Iterate and Refine: Even the biggest ideas need shaping and refining. Be prepared to iterate on your concept, testing and tweaking until it resonates.

The Impact of Big Ideas

The impact of Big Ideas extends far beyond the immediate success of a marketing campaign. They can propel brands into the realm of icons, create movements, and even influence societal norms. From Nike's "Just Do It" to Apple's "Think Different," Big Ideas have not only defined brands but also inspired generations.

In the quest for fame and fortune, as Ogilvy suggests, the invention of Big Ideas is paramount. It's about daring to dream big, to envision what others haven't, and to bring those visions to life in a way that captivates and compels. The journey towards discovering your Big Idea is challenging, fraught with risks and uncertainties, but it's also the most rewarding path for those brave enough to walk it. In the end, the Big Idea is what distinguishes the leaders from the followers, the remembered from the forgotten.

Offer

The offer is one of the most important parts of your copy.
A good offer is the cornerstone of effective marketing and sales efforts. It's the catalyst that transforms interest into action, nudging potential customers from contemplation to purchase. Understanding the importance of a good offer and mastering the art of writing one can significantly boost your business's success. Here's why a compelling offer is crucial and how you can craft one:

Importance of a Good Offer

Drives Conversions: A compelling offer can tip the scales in your favor, converting prospects into customers. It's the difference between someone considering your product or service and actually making the decision to purchase.

- ☞ Increases Perceived Value: A good offer adds perceived value to your proposition without necessarily increasing your costs. By presenting your products or services alongside additional benefits, you make the choice to purchase more attractive and urgent.

- ☞ Differentiates from Competitors: In a crowded market, your offer can set you apart from competitors. A unique or particularly valuable offer draws attention and can be a key reason customers choose you over others.
- ☞ Encourages Immediate Action: By incorporating elements of scarcity or time sensitivity, a strong offer creates a sense of urgency, encouraging prospects to act now rather than later, which can significantly boost your sales momentum.
- ☞ Builds Customer Loyalty: First-time customers attracted by an irresistible offer are more likely to have a positive perception of your brand, leading to higher chances of repeat business and long-term loyalty.

How to Write a Good Offer

Crafting a compelling offer involves more than just slashing prices or bundling products. It requires strategic thinking and an understanding of your target audience's needs and desires. Here's how to write an offer that resonates and converts:

- ☞ Know Your Audience: Understand the problems, needs, and desires of your target audience. A good offer addresses these directly, presenting your product or service as the solution.
- ☞ Highlight the Value: Focus on the value your product or service provides, not just the features. Explain how it makes your customers' lives better, easier, or more enjoyable.
- ☞ Add Bonuses or Extras: Enhance the attractiveness of your offer by including bonuses, free gifts, or additional services. These should complement the main offering and add real value.
- ☞ Create a Sense of Urgency: Use time-limited offers or limited quantities to encourage quick decisions. Phrases like "Offer ends soon," "While supplies last," or "Limited time offer" can motivate immediate action.
- ☞ Make It Clear and Simple: Your offer should be easy to understand at a glance. Complicated offers with too many conditions or steps can deter potential customers.

- ☞ Ensure It's Compelling: Your offer should feel like a no-brainer to your target audience. The value should far outweigh the cost, making the decision to purchase easy.
- ☞ Test and Refine: Use A/B testing to try out different offers and see which ones resonate most with your audience. Continuously refine your offer based on feedback and performance metrics.
- ☞ Communicate the Offer Effectively: Use clear, persuasive language to communicate your offer through your marketing channels. Ensure that the message is consistent across all platforms, from your website to your social media.

A well-crafted offer can make all the difference in your marketing and sales efforts, turning passive interest into active purchases and long-term customer relationships. By understanding your audience, emphasizing value, and creating a sense of urgency, you can create offers that not only attract attention but also drive significant business growth.

More About Carl Galletti

Carl Galletti is a freelance copywriter, author, speaker, coach, and direct response marketing expert specializing in email, sales pages, and blog posts. Each week he writes up to 20 emails, including two newsletters – one on marketing and another on artificial intelligence – that go out to as many as 450,000 people.

His affiliate sales accomplishments include $54,835.00 in sales within an 18-hour period with a list of less than 5,000; another $106,287.00 within a 24-hour period; $38,883.00 in 16 days; and numerous other sales using email as an affiliate.

Weekly sales from his emails average in the $30,000.00 to $50,000.00 range and occasionally reach as high as ten times that amount.

His sales letters have sold millions of dollars' worth of client products and he has personally coached hundreds of copywriting students through his Copywriter Protégé program.

His consultations with clients have resulted in as much as an extra $503,417.00 per month due to his recommendations.

His personal best is $458,949.00 in sales as a result of a 60-minute presentation to a few hundred people.

Carl has been a sought after freelance direct response copywriter/marketer for more than 37 years and has been trained by Gary Halbert, Jay Abraham, Joe Sugarman, Tom Collins, Gary Bencivenga, and other direct marketing legends.

You can find a treasure trove of his recommended marketing books, audios, and videos at: ScientificAdvertising.com, CopyCoach.com, and CarlGalletti.com.

Chapter 5

Ethical and Responsible Marketing

"To build a long-term, successful enterprise, when you don't close a sale, open a relationship."

~ Patricia Fripp

Tell someone you're a marketer and you'll be met with any of several reactions. These will include but are not limited to a gasp, accompanied by raised eyebrows, a gaping mouth wide open and eyes staring a hole into your heart, and a crooked smile with a furrowed brow.

These were all reactions from people who knew and liked me, at least until I uttered the "M" word regarding the work I was now doing.

You will discover that many people admire and also highly respect marketers, but in my experience, they tend to be individuals who are more interested in the theory of marketing, and not so much in the day-to-day application of the principles.

I was initially drawn to marketing because of the effectiveness with which you could sell almost anything, as long as you sufficiently made the case as to why someone needed whatever you were offering, and right now. This part is about urgency and scarcity, strategies that work well if they are presented properly and believable by your prospects.

For marketing to be effective long-term, it must be honest and transparent. It's too easy and sometimes tempting for people to inflate their experiences instead of sticking with the truth. This leads to marketing that is the polar opposite of being ethical and responsible.

One thing I have loved about the internet since starting my online business in 2006 is the fact that our lives are an open book. Yes, we can keep our private lives out of the public eye to some extent, but most of what we do and have done in years past is just a Google search away.

I continue to use post office boxes to receive mail in both of the cities I call home, yet a diligent search will most likely lead to a physical address. While I am not hiding anything I do not want others to know, I have become more diligent in protecting my privacy.

I'm active in both of my cities with volunteering, fundraising, and charitable work, and the details of what I'm involved with are readily available online. In fact, I like to do the marketing for all of this myself. Why? This way people who search for me on Google and elsewhere will find enough to satisfy their curiosity, without delving deeper into my private life.

In other words, be willing to give others, no matter who these people might be a chance to know something about you that will be congruent with who you are and how you present yourself to the world, while not giving anyone access to your home address or phone number.

Your Message

You have a message that needs to be shared. Whether you already know without a shadow of a doubt what that message is, or if you are still in the process of identifying it and putting it into words and other modalities, it's there.

I encourage you to dig deep into your soul to discover the message that you want and need to share. Remember, there are people all over the world who need to hear your message, and the majority of them will only be able to hear this message from you. Why? Because your message is a personal one and will affect others, the likes of which you may not be able to fully understand today.

And remember, even when your message has a negative aspect, share your thoughts and ideas and then be sure to include the positive side, or at least your take on it that can be reframed. I too often read email messages and blog posts that are filled with complaints, yet offer no sign that anything was learned from what occurred or is still an issue. Entrepreneurs and marketers are problem solvers, so this will always be an opportunity to show and explain to others how you were able to turn everything around in some way.

Marketing is Intended to Open a Relationship

Many people will tell you that they bristle at the very thought of the idea of marketing. When I encounter someone who verbally or visually feels this way, I probe more deeply to find out more. This type of research continues to make a difference in the way I market in my business, as well as how I interact with others in my life on a daily basis.

Marketing is almost always perceived initially as someone wanting to sell us something. People have described to me how they feel when someone is attempting to talk them into buying something they do not want or do not have the money to purchase.

When I ask them to use words and phrases to describe this feeling to me, these may include "icky", "dirty", "disgusting", "intimidating", "like I was being pursued as prey", "it felt like they only cared about making a sale", "insulting to my intelligence", and "not about me or what would be appropriate for me in the situation."

I can empathize with these feelings and perceptions, as I have been in the same situation many times over the years. But now that I consider myself to be a professional marketer and someone who is quite effective with my strategies and actions, I go out of my way to make sure the people I encounter are not left with a bad taste in their mouths, but instead a feeling of being served and cared for in a way that is honest and sincere.

It all comes down to this... Marketing is intended to open a relationship, not to close a sale.

When you think of marketing in this way, it's a joyous process to start a conversation with the premise that you are getting to know someone better, and therefore, to be able to serve them in the process.

And just as marketing at its best will open relationships, the opposite will also be true when there is a lapse of judgment or understanding by one party or another.

I recently ended an almost twenty-year relationship with a veterinarian. After he or the other vets working in his office had cared for over a dozen of my animals, including dogs, cats, and even a snake, a single incident changed everything.

The man who has owned this animal hospital for over forty years began hiring vets and technicians on a part-time basis as he got closer to retirement. I had the misfortune of dealing with someone who, in my opinion, was unfit to care for or even be around animals. My pet survived the incident but was traumatized in the process.

When I contacted the veterinarian, I had known for so long and had trusted to only hire the most caring, compassionate, and knowledgeable veterinarians to work in his office, he would not take my call. In a short email response, he said that he stood behind the man who caused the problem and that I was to blame for not agreeing to have thousands of dollars in additional tests done at the time.

This is now a legal matter, and his attempts at ramping up his marketing campaigns to get more clients after so many people other than myself also had negative experiences and have taken their pets elsewhere are not effective.

One or two bad reviews from disgruntled clients are one thing, but when it becomes obvious there is a problem and some of the issues go viral on social media and end up going to litigation, the person's reputation is ruined and they are effectively put out of business.

Not only have I ended this relationship permanently, but in conversations with people we have in common because of our volunteer work in the community, I've discovered that there are many other areas and situations that are questionable with this person.

Relational vs Transactional

Looking back over jobs I've had over the decades, I was already choosing the "relational" approach over the "transactional", many times to the chagrin of those I was working for in that capacity.

I've sold cars twice in my life experience. The first time was right after I graduated from UCLA and was taking a year off before heading off to law school.

We had decided to return to Miami, as a way to spend time with friends and family we hadn't seen very often while I was in college in Los Angeles. We rented an apartment not far from the beach and I scanned the classified ads in The Miami Herald to see what was available.

The Toyota dealership was almost within walking distance and they were looking for salespeople. After a less than ten-minute interview, they hired me.

The General Manager of this dealership was a man named Louie. He was from New Jersey and I loved how he spoke. I can't describe it here well enough to do justice to him, but his style of speaking and dealing with people was literal, abrupt, and to the point, without ever being rude or condescending.

Instead of turning people off with this demeanor, Louie disarmed everyone he came into contact with and made them feel like he was their best friend. He was a born salesman and when he took me under his wing, I felt cared for and very special as a brand-new salesperson.

While we waited for prospective customers to show up in the parking lot, we would role-play different scenarios.

He'd pretend to be a doctor, a housewife, a college student, or a newly married couple. It was hilarious to watch and hear him in action. Somehow, I knew that what he was teaching me, and anyone else who would take the time to be a part of this impromptu training would serve me as valuable knowledge for many years to come. Everyone is a salesman, yet only the most caring and astute individuals will make it a goal to learn how to add sales and persuasion to their repertoire of marketing strategies.

Positioning Your Products in an Honest and Ethical Way

At this point in my career as a marketer, I can sell just about anything to almost anybody. This is based on the skills I have acquired over the years and the practice with these skills I continue to hone throughout each day in my business.

But just because you can do something, doesn't mean that you should do it. In my thinking, it's all black and white and there is no gray area here. Deep down inside, you know if something is right or wrong, regardless of whether it is legal or not.

I like sales trainer and coach Phil M. Jones' definition of selling: "Selling is earning the right to make a recommendation."

Chapter 6

Marketing for Others as a Business Model

"When you support small businesses, what you're really supporting is a dream."

~ Jerry Greenfield, co-founder of Ben & Jerry's

Early on in my quest to become an online entrepreneur, I came up with the idea to help a family member by practicing what I was learning for my own business for his benefit as well.

Erik was a handyman by trade and had recently relocated to a city about thirty miles from where he had been living for several years. His goal was to start fresh in the new community and avoid commuting back to the area where he had worked previously.

It had all sounded doable until his move was complete. Now he wasn't so sure he could find new customers so easily for a variety of reasons.

His initial solution was to run newspaper and magazine advertisements, and he had called to ask me if I thought a radio spot might be helpful.

I agreed to meet with Erik and he brought a copy of the local newspaper and the magazine where he was paying for ads.

What he had written was fine. But fine doesn't make the phone ring. Instead, we must be more creative with our marketing. That was exactly what I was learning and implementing each day as a new online entrepreneur and marketer, so I offered to help him.

Our agreement was a simple one; I would set up a blog and join some local online forums on his behalf and market for him at no cost for the next sixty days. Social media was in its infancy in 2006 and 2007, so we didn't even discuss this aspect of the marketing I would be doing on his behalf. At the end of the sixty days, we would again meet in person and review the results. This would determine if I would continue to do this work for him at an agreed-upon fee, or if I would stop altogether and he would continue to pay for newspaper, magazine, and local radio advertising.

I went to work almost immediately, after doing some research to find out who his competitors were and how they were marketing themselves and their businesses.

No one else had a blog, but this did not come as a surprise. Blogs and blogging were new concepts in 2006 and had not yet caught on among small business owners. I had Erik purchase a dot com domain that included his city and the phrase "handyman service." I was just starting to learn about search engine optimization (SEO) and knew the combination of the location and the industry in the domain name, as long as it was a dot com (.com) would make a world of difference.

Writing simple blog posts about the various work he did – he wasn't a general contractor, so he was limited with what he could do for others) was simple for me, and I even found someone online who was selling private label rights (PLR) content on topics around home repair.

Next, I joined a local real estate forum called Active Rain, where I could share these blog posts and his name and contact information.

At this time, I had just begun going to the Rotary Club for their weekly meetings, and I asked the members where they recommended someone advertise for a new local business. They suggested the Chamber of Commerce, but I didn't think Erik's business was appropriate for that. He was working from home and using his garage as his workspace.

Someone also mentioned a weekly meeting of small business owners, and Erik and I attended the following week. It was a breakfast meeting at the local IHOP (International House of Pancakes) and the meeting was called to order promptly at 7 a.m.

Long story short, there were contractors in this group who did not like the idea of a handyman coming into their group. When the meeting had concluded, Erik filled out the paperwork to join. He was told that he would be contacted before the next scheduled meeting if he had been approved.

Several days later, Erik called to tell me that his membership request had been turned down. The plumber, electrician, and HVAC (heating, ventilation, and air conditioning) contractors felt it would take business away from them if he joined. The lady who called Erik even told her that one of the contractors said he was "too nice" and that customers would gravitate towards him. This was funny, but I could tell he was hurt by the rejection.

I didn't discuss this with him further, but several months later someone in the community told me that Erik was regularly recommending these contractors to people he encountered who needed work done. He asked me why he would do this. My answer was a simple one:

> *"Erik is a handyman, not a licensed contractor, so it makes sense that he would recommend people he had met in person who were qualified to do the work that was needed. And besides, he's getting so many calls from people who need a handyman, he's thinking of hiring a couple of helpers."*

The man I was speaking with on that day could read between the lines; Erik's phone was ringing because of the marketing I was still doing for him, now as a paid marketing strategist.

I've written a book on this topic, titled *Small Business Marketing: Making the Phone Ring for Businesses Everywhere* if you are interested in helping small businesses as a part-time side hustle or as a full-time business endeavor.

Chapter 7

Emotional Intelligence and the Art of Persuasion with Miguel A. de Jesús

"Emotional Intelligence grows through perception. Look around at your present situation and observe it through the level of feeling."

~ Deepak Chopra

When I realized that no book on the topic of marketing would be complete without a thorough discussion around emotional intelligence and persuasion, I immediately thought of my friend, colleague, and mentor Miguel A. de Jesús.

Miguel is a thought leader, a consummate professional, and an expert and authority on both emotional intelligence and the art of persuasion. He kindly agreed to write this chapter, adding his expertise in a way that no one else could.

Emotional Intelligence and the Art of Persuasion: Self-Discovery Skills to Become a Better Marketer

by Miguel A. de Jesús

Visit your values – check in with your- self and your core beliefs for how you want to live your life. See if you can describe how each value is visible in your daily life; and if it's not, what can you do to change that?

A fundamental cornerstone of emotional intelligence is understanding what your emotional triggers are and where they came from, so you can modify or neutralize them. You want to be a good leader and set a good example both at home and at work.

That is why we first focus on self-aware-ness, digging deeply into who you are at the core, and finding out how you got that way. That's all becoming self-aware truly is about getting to know who you are as a human being.

You're going to peel back the layers of the onion one at a time and discover things that will impress you about yourself as well as discover things that might surprise you that you're not so happy about.

As you learn more and more about yourself, you can gradually take control of your emotions and therefore your life. Your relationships will improve as will your work environment.

So, let's get going and discuss six skills that will help you to understand yourself and your emotions better and therefore have a happier and more successful life and improve your leadership skills.

Understanding How Your Emotions Impact Others Around You

Have you ever noticed people at work who order people around and are impatient when the assigned task isn't done perfectly? Some people think that a sign of being a great leader is, essentially, being a stern bully, not realizing that it simply kills confidence, self-esteem, and loyalty.

That's why it's important to discuss this Emotional Intelligence skill, to put it into perspective so you will want to learn more about controlling or neutralizing some of those negative emotions and utilizing the positive emotions that not only benefit others but help you reach your own goals as well. We must always take emotions into consideration as we go through our daily lives.

Negative Emotion

When you are angry with someone and let them know it ... the person feels bad and resents you.

It's unpleasant for you because you probably get angry every time you think of the incident, and those in proximity feel bad.

All in all, it makes you not very popular, not respected; and in the workplace, for example, no one wants to try their best around you because they don't want to incur your wrath. They do just what needs to be done to avoid any confrontation with you and nothing more.

The same thing happens at home. That one outburst doesn't just affect you or the one you directed your anger at, but everyone who was there, whether they're family members or just friends visiting.

Positive Emotion

Of course, on the other side of the coin, when you're happy, respectful, and supportive, it has the same ripple effect from person to person, just like when you throw a pebble into a pond. These are the types of emotional ripples you want to create in your life.

Positive emotions draw people toward you, make them like (and sometimes love) and respect and trust you, and strengthen your relationships with them ... everyone from a significant other or child to a coworker or business partner.

The Power of Emotions

Emotions are powerful. They can be a powerful weapon to use against others and push them away or a powerful draw that brings loyalty, respect, and love into your life. Either way, it can affect which direction your relationships go and whether you can reach your goals.

We will now begin to determine which great empowering emotions come naturally to you as well as which negative emotions come naturally to you so you can create strategies to enhance the emotions you want to keep and at least modify, if not neutralize, the ones that are holding you back.

Some people think you must be a stern bully to be a great leader, not realizing that it simply kills confidence, self-esteem, and loyalty in others.

At work or home, negative emotions can destroy relationships and affect even those who are just observing the outburst.

Positive emotions create happiness, respect, and trust, and strengthen your relationships.

Emotions are powerful weapons that can destroy relationships and make your goals less attainable, or can launch you into a future of success and happiness.

Keep an "Emotion" Journal To Learn About Yourself

Do yourself a favor and do this exercise. It can change your life. And it's fun! You don't have to be a great writer. You don't have to be a writer at all! (See our tips below for those who hate writing.)

This isn't a literary exercise. It's a "learning about you" exercise that will reveal patterns that you want to improve upon and patterns you will probably want to change.

Yes, change takes motivation and effort, but the rewards can be exhilarating. Some changes can save your relationship, save your job, and improve your life.

But the first step is to find out what's working for you and what's working against you.

A regular journal is simply a story of your life that many people keep for years, commenting on things that happen throughout the day, how they feel about it, and maybe including thoughts about the future ... goals, hopes, and dreams. It's simply a chat with yourself that no one but you will ever read.

An "Emotion" Journal focuses more on how you feel and react throughout the day, so you can discover what triggers happy emotions, sad emotions, and sometimes out-of-control emotions. Commit to doing this for 30 days. You don't have to do it forever (although you can if you find it enjoyable; many people do).

- ☞ Get a spiral-bound notebook and carry it with you throughout the day. At the top of the first page, put the date and day.
- ☞ Beginning with when you get up in the morning, be aware of your moods, and your emotions.
- ☞ Did you wake up in a bad mood, resenting the fact that you have to go to a job that you don't like?
- ☞ Were you grumpy with your family as a result?
- ☞ Did you have a nice breakfast that made you happy?
- ☞ Did someone make that nice breakfast for you? How did you feel about that? Did you show how much you appreciated it? Or just take it for granted?
- ☞ Were you late for work because you overslept?
- ☞ Did you take that out on your family and coworkers?
- ☞ Or did you wake up enthusiastically anticipating a wonderful new day?

- ☞ Did you make your significant other or family laugh and feel happy you were there, thus getting their days off to a positive start?
- ☞ Monitor your emotions carefully. They will be a big part of your day. By the end of the day, you will already have an insight as to which emotions are serving you well, and which emotions are sabotaging you.
- ☞ Then analyze each emotion.
- ☞ Were you angry because your ego said something must be done exactly your way without asking for the other person's feedback?
- ☞ Did you act like a bully by dictating orders in a rude way rather than requesting a project be done and then being appreciative?

Unlocking Your Marketing Potential: Leveraging Emotional Intelligence, Leadership, and Persuasion

Embarking on the journey of online entrepreneurship demands more than just business acumen—it requires a deep understanding of oneself and the art of persuasion. In the realm of digital commerce, success hinges not only on the products or services you offer but also on your ability to connect with your audience on a human level. Let's delve into the realm of emotional intelligence, leadership, and persuasion to unearth the keys to becoming a more effective marketer.

Explore Your Core Values

Before diving headlong into marketing strategies, take a moment to reconnect with your values. Reflect on what truly drives you and aligns with your vision for your online venture. Consider how these values manifest in your daily interactions and endeavors. Are they evident in your branding, messaging, and customer interactions? If not, ponder ways to infuse them more authentically into your business approach.

Master Self-Awareness

At the heart of emotional intelligence lies self-awareness—the ability to recognize and understand your own emotions and triggers. As an online entrepreneur, honing this skill is paramount. Delve deep into your psyche to uncover the roots of your emotional responses and behaviors. By gaining clarity on your inner workings, you can exert greater control over your reactions and navigate challenges with composure and foresight.

Understand Emotional Impact

In the digital landscape, your emotions reverberate far beyond your own experience—they ripple outward, shaping perceptions and influencing outcomes. Consider the ramifications of negative emotions such as impatience or anger in your interactions with customers or team members.

Recognize that these emotions not only erode trust and morale but also detract from your effectiveness as a marketer. Conversely, harness the power of positivity to foster connection, inspire loyalty, and propel your brand forward.

Harness the Power of Persuasion

As an online entrepreneur, persuasion is your currency. Recognize that effective persuasion isn't about coercion or manipulation—it's about building genuine rapport and guiding others toward shared objectives. Cultivate empathy and active listening skills to understand your audience's needs and desires.

Craft compelling narratives that resonate with their emotions and aspirations, compelling them to engage with your brand and offerings.

Keep an "Emotion" Journal

I mentioned this previously, but this exercise is important enough to bear repeating, albeit from a slightly different perspective. So, you may deepen your understanding of yourself and refine your marketing approach, consider keeping an "Emotion" Journal. Document your daily experiences, noting the emotions they evoke and the triggers behind them. By meticulously tracking your emotional landscape, you can identify patterns, strengths, and areas for growth. Armed with this insight, you can tailor your marketing strategies to resonate more authentically with your target audience.

In the realm of online entrepreneurship, success is not solely determined by product quality or market saturation—it's shaped by the depth of your emotional intelligence, the strength of your leadership, and the artistry of your persuasion. Embrace these self-discovery skills as pillars of your marketing prowess, and watch as your online venture flourishes in the digital arena.

What about the connection between emotional intelligence and the art of persuasion in marketing...

Unlocking the Power of Emotional Intelligence: Elevating the Art of Persuasion in Marketing

In the fast-paced world of marketing, where trends shift with lightning speed and consumer attention is a prized commodity, mastering the art of persuasion is essential for success. Yet, amidst the ceaseless chatter of digital platforms and the ever-evolving landscape of consumer preferences, one often overlooked aspect stands as a potent force: emotional intelligence.

Understanding and harnessing the power of emotions can be the key differentiator in crafting compelling marketing campaigns that resonate deeply with audiences and drive impactful results.

At its core, emotional intelligence (EI) refers to the ability to recognize, understand, and manage both our own emotions and those of others. It encompasses self-awareness, self-regulation, empathy, and social skills—qualities that are invaluable in the realm of persuasion. When applied effectively, EI enables marketers to forge genuine connections with their target audience, tap into their deepest desires and motivations, and ultimately influence their behavior in meaningful ways.

So, what is the connection between emotional intelligence and the art of persuasion in marketing?

Empathy as a Foundation

Empathy lies at the heart of emotional intelligence and serves as the cornerstone of persuasive marketing. By empathizing with their audience, marketers can gain profound insights into their needs, preferences, and pain points. This empathic understanding forms the basis for creating marketing messages that resonate on a visceral level, demonstrating a genuine understanding of and concern for the audience's well-being.

Crafting Compelling Narratives

Effective persuasion hinges on storytelling—the art of weaving narratives that captivate the imagination, evoke emotions, and spur action. Marketers with a high degree of emotional intelligence possess an innate ability to craft narratives that resonate with their audience's emotions, aspirations, and values.

By tapping into universal human experiences and emotions such as joy, fear, love, and belonging, they can create narratives that forge deep emotional connections and compel audiences to engage with their brand.

Navigating Emotional Triggers

Emotions can be powerful drivers of behavior, shaping our perceptions, decisions, and actions. Marketers with a keen understanding of emotional intelligence are adept at navigating the complex terrain of emotional triggers.

Whether it's addressing fears and anxieties, tapping into aspirations and desires, or evoking feelings of nostalgia and belonging, they can leverage emotional triggers to elicit desired responses from their audience.

Adapting to Cultural Sensitivities

In an increasingly globalized world, cultural sensitivity is essential in persuasive marketing. Emotional intelligence enables marketers to navigate cultural nuances and sensitivities with finesse, ensuring that their messages resonate authentically with diverse audiences.

By understanding the cultural context in which their audience operates and tailoring their approach accordingly, marketers can avoid inadvertently causing offense or alienating potential customers.

In conclusion, emotional intelligence serves as a powerful ally in the art of persuasion in marketing. By cultivating empathy, crafting compelling narratives, building trust, navigating emotional triggers, and adapting to cultural sensitivities, marketers can elevate their persuasion skills to new heights.

In a crowded marketplace where attention is scarce and competition is fierce, the ability to connect with audiences on an emotional level can spell the difference between success and obscurity.

As marketers continue to navigate the ever-evolving landscape of digital marketing, embracing emotional intelligence as a guiding principle can unlock untold opportunities for growth, engagement, and influence.

How marketers can use the power of persuasion to build relationships and make more sales, especially online.

Mastering the Art of Persuasion: Building Relationships and Driving Sales in the Digital Era

In the bustling realm of online commerce, where competition is fierce and consumer attention is fleeting, the ability to persuade and connect with potential customers is paramount. While traditional sales tactics may have once relied heavily on aggressive pitches and relentless promotion, the digital landscape demands a more nuanced approach—one rooted in building genuine relationships and fostering trust.

Here, we explore how marketers can harness the power of persuasion to cultivate meaningful connections and drive sales in the ever-evolving world of e-commerce.

Understand Your Audience

Effective persuasion begins with a deep understanding of your target audience. Take the time to research and analyze your customers' demographics, preferences, and pain points. What are their needs and desires? What challenges are they facing? By gaining insights into your audience's motivations and aspirations, you can tailor your messaging and offerings to resonate more deeply with their interests and concerns.

Craft Compelling Content

Content is king in the digital age, and compelling storytelling is a potent tool for persuasion. Whether through blog posts, social media updates, or video content, strive to create engaging narratives that captivate your audience's attention and evoke emotion. Share stories that highlight the benefits of your products or services in a relatable and authentic manner. By providing value and entertainment through your content, you can establish trust and credibility with your audience, laying the foundation for lasting relationships.

Leverage Social Proof

Humans are social creatures, and we tend to look to others for guidance and validation. Harness the power of social proof by showcasing testimonials, reviews, and user-generated content that highlight the positive experiences of satisfied customers. By demonstrating that others have found value in your offerings, you can alleviate doubts and instill confidence in prospective buyers, making them more likely to convert.

Cultivate Engagement and Interaction

Building relationships in the digital realm requires active engagement and interaction with your audience. Encourage dialogue and conversation through social media, email marketing, and live chat platforms. Respond promptly to inquiries, address customer concerns, and solicit feedback to demonstrate that you value their input and opinions. By fostering a sense of community and belonging, you can forge stronger connections with your audience and keep them coming back for more.

Personalize the Experience

In the era of big data and machine learning, personalization has become a cornerstone of effective marketing. Leverage customer data and analytics to deliver personalized experiences tailored to the individual preferences and behaviors of your audience.

From personalized product recommendations to targeted email campaigns, customization allows you to speak directly to the needs and interests of each customer, enhancing the likelihood of conversion and retention.

Offer Value Beyond the Sale

Successful relationships are built on mutual trust and reciprocity. Instead of focusing solely on making a sale, strive to provide ongoing value to your customers even after they've made a purchase. Offer educational resources, exclusive discounts, or loyalty rewards to incentivize repeat business and foster loyalty. By demonstrating that you're invested in their success and well-being, you can turn one-time buyers into lifelong advocates for your brand.

As you now see, the digital age presents both challenges and opportunities for marketers seeking to build relationships and drive sales online. By harnessing the power of persuasion through audience understanding, compelling content, social proof, engagement, personalization, and ongoing value delivery, marketers can cultivate meaningful connections with their audience and drive sustainable growth in the competitive landscape of e-commerce.

As technology continues to evolve and consumer expectations shift, embracing these principles of persuasion will be essential for success in the digital era.

Learning more about emotional intelligence can be helpful to entrepreneurs in their marketing strategies, and how this leads to improved relationships both personally and professionally.

Unlocking Success: How Emotional Intelligence Empowers Entrepreneurs in Marketing and Beyond

In the dynamic world of entrepreneurship, success hinges not only on innovative ideas and strategic acumen but also on the ability to navigate the complex terrain of human emotions. As entrepreneurs strive to build thriving businesses and forge meaningful connections with their audience, mastering the principles of emotional intelligence (EI) emerges as a crucial skill set.

Here, we explore how learning more about emotional intelligence can be a game-changer for entrepreneurs, enhancing their marketing strategies and fostering improved relationships both personally and professionally.

Understanding Emotional Intelligence

Emotional intelligence encompasses a spectrum of skills, including self-awareness, self-regulation, empathy, social skills, and relationship management. At its core, EI involves the ability to recognize, understand, and manage one's own emotions, as well as the emotions of others.

For entrepreneurs, developing emotional intelligence is instrumental in navigating the myriad challenges of building and growing a business. From negotiating deals and managing teams to engaging with customers and stakeholders, EI underpins every aspect of entrepreneurial success.

Enhanced Marketing Strategies

In the realm of marketing, emotional intelligence serves as a potent tool for connecting with audiences on a deeper level. By understanding the emotional drivers and motivations of their target market, entrepreneurs can craft more resonant and compelling marketing messages.

For example, empathizing with the pain points and desires of their audience allows entrepreneurs to tailor their marketing content to address specific needs and aspirations. By evoking emotions such as joy, fear, or nostalgia, marketers can create memorable campaigns that leave a lasting impression on consumers.

Moreover, emotional intelligence enables entrepreneurs to cultivate authenticity and trust in their branding efforts. By expressing genuine empathy and understanding in their communications, entrepreneurs can foster stronger connections with their audience, building brand loyalty and advocacy over time.

Improved Personal and Professional Relationships

Beyond marketing, emotional intelligence also plays a pivotal role in fostering positive relationships both personally and professionally. Entrepreneurs who possess high levels of EI are better equipped to navigate interpersonal dynamics, resolve conflicts, and inspire collaboration among team members.

By cultivating empathy and active listening skills, entrepreneurs can forge deeper connections with their employees, fostering a culture of trust, respect, and mutual support within their organization. This, in turn, leads to higher levels of employee satisfaction, productivity, and retention.

Moreover, emotional intelligence enhances entrepreneurs' ability to build rapport with clients, investors, and other stakeholders. By understanding and addressing their needs and concerns, entrepreneurs can foster stronger partnerships and drive business growth through meaningful collaborations.

You now understand that learning more about emotional intelligence holds immense value for entrepreneurs seeking to thrive in the competitive landscape of business. By leveraging EI to inform their marketing strategies and enhance their interpersonal skills, entrepreneurs can unlock new opportunities for growth and success.

Whether forging connections with customers, leading teams, or nurturing professional relationships, emotional intelligence serves as a guiding beacon for entrepreneurial achievement in the modern era.

Can someone new to marketing become a master of the art of persuasion, even if they are new to entrepreneurship and marketing?

Someone new to marketing can indeed become a master of the art of persuasion, regardless of their prior experience in entrepreneurship or marketing. While expertise and years of practice certainly contribute to mastery, the key lies in dedication, willingness to learn, and consistent effort. Here's how:

Study and Learn: Begin by immersing yourself in the principles of persuasion and marketing. There are countless resources available, from books and online courses to podcasts and webinars. Take advantage of these resources to gain a solid understanding of the fundamental concepts and techniques of persuasion.

Practice, Practice, Practice: Like any skill, mastering persuasion requires practice. Start by applying what you've learned in real-world scenarios, whether it's crafting persuasive messages, delivering compelling presentations, or engaging with potential customers. Don't be afraid to experiment and refine your approach based on feedback and results.

Seek Mentorship and Guidance

Surround yourself with experienced marketers and entrepreneurs who can offer valuable insights and mentorship. Learn from their experiences, ask questions, and seek advice on how to improve your persuasion skills. Networking within the marketing community can also provide valuable opportunities for growth and learning.

Stay Curious and Open-Minded

The field of marketing is constantly evolving, with new technologies, trends, and strategies emerging regularly. Stay curious and keep abreast of industry developments by reading industry publications, attending conferences, and participating in online forums. Be open-minded and willing to adapt your approach as needed to stay ahead of the curve.

Seek Feedback and Learn from Mistakes

Don't be discouraged by setbacks or failures along the way. Instead, view them as opportunities for growth and learning. Solicit feedback from peers, mentors, and customers, and use it to identify areas for improvement. Reflect on your experiences, analyze what worked well and what didn't, and use those insights to refine your approach moving forward.

Embrace Continuous Learning

Mastery is a journey, not a destination. Even seasoned marketers are continually learning and refining their skills. Commit to lifelong learning and continuous improvement, whether it's through further education, professional development opportunities, or simply staying curious and engaged with the field.

While becoming a master of persuasion in marketing may seem daunting for someone new to the field, keep in mind that this goal is entirely achievable with dedication, perseverance, and a willingness to learn. By studying the principles of persuasion, practicing consistently, seeking mentorship, staying curious, and embracing feedback, aspiring marketers can develop the skills and expertise needed to excel in the art of persuasion, regardless of their background or experience level.

How do we define persuasion, in terms of sales and marketing?

In the context of sales and marketing, persuasion can be defined as the deliberate effort to influence someone's beliefs, attitudes, or behaviors to achieve a desired outcome, typically to make a sale or promote a product, service, or idea. It involves using various techniques and strategies to appeal to the emotions, logic, or values of the target audience to convince them to take a particular action or make a specific decision.

Persuasion in Sales and Marketing Involves More Than is Obvious to the Casual Observer

Understanding the Audience: Persuasion begins with a deep understanding of the target audience—their needs, preferences, motivations, and pain points. Marketers must tailor their messaging and approach to resonate with the specific desires and concerns of their audience.

Building Credibility and Trust

Trust is a foundational element of persuasion. Marketers must establish credibility and build trust with their audience by demonstrating expertise, authenticity, and transparency. Testimonials, reviews, and endorsements can help bolster credibility and instill confidence in the brand or product.

Creating Compelling Messages

Persuasive messages are crafted to capture attention, evoke emotion, and convey the benefits of the product or service compellingly. Marketers use storytelling, imagery, and persuasive language to engage the audience and persuade them to take action.

Addressing Objections

Effective persuasion involves anticipating and addressing potential objections or concerns that may arise in the minds of the audience. Marketers must proactively overcome objections by providing solutions, addressing doubts, and highlighting the value proposition of the offering.

Creating a Sense of Urgency

Persuasion often relies on creating a sense of urgency or scarcity to prompt immediate action. Limited-time offers, exclusive deals, or countdown timers can motivate consumers to act quickly to avoid missing out on a valuable opportunity.

Engaging Emotions

Emotions play a powerful role in decision-making. Persuasive marketing often taps into emotions such as joy, fear, excitement, or nostalgia to create a strong emotional connection with the audience and drive desired actions.

In summary, persuasion in sales and marketing involves understanding the audience, building trust and credibility, creating compelling messages, addressing objections, leveraging social proof, creating a sense of urgency, and engaging emotions to influence behavior and achieve desired outcomes.

Could a basic understanding of emotional intelligence be both helpful and effective as a strategy when marketers are engaged in sales, persuasion, and marketing of their products, courses, and services?

Absolutely, a basic understanding of emotional intelligence (EI) can be tremendously helpful and effective for marketers engaged in sales, persuasion, and marketing of their products, courses, and services. Here's how:

Building Rapport

Emotional intelligence enables marketers to build rapport and connect with their audience on a deeper level. By empathizing with their customers' needs, concerns, and aspirations, marketers can tailor their messaging and approach to resonate more authentically with their target audience.

Understanding Customer Emotions

Emotional intelligence allows marketers to better understand the emotions and motivations driving their customers' purchasing decisions. By recognizing and addressing customers' emotional triggers and pain points, marketers can craft more compelling and persuasive messages that resonate with their audience on an emotional level.

Enhancing Communication

Effective communication is a cornerstone of successful marketing. Emotional intelligence enables marketers to communicate more effectively by recognizing and managing their own emotions, as well as understanding and responding to the emotions of others. By expressing empathy, active listening, and clear communication, marketers can foster stronger connections with their audience and build trust and credibility.

Resolving Objections

In sales and marketing, objections are a common hurdle that must be overcome. Emotional intelligence equips marketers with the skills to handle objections tactfully and empathetically.

By understanding the underlying emotions behind customers' objections, marketers can address their concerns in a way that alleviates doubts and builds confidence in the product or service being offered.

Creating Emotional Connections

Emotional intelligence enables marketers to create emotional connections with their audience, which can be a powerful driver of brand loyalty and customer engagement. By tapping into customers' emotions such as joy, excitement, or nostalgia, marketers can create memorable experiences that resonate with their audience and inspire loyalty and advocacy.

Adapting to Feedback

Emotional intelligence allows marketers to receive and respond to feedback more effectively. By remaining open-minded, receptive, and non-defensive, marketers can use feedback as an opportunity for growth and improvement. Whether it's positive feedback or constructive criticism, emotional intelligence enables marketers to adapt and evolve their strategies in response to customer feedback.

You can now see that a basic understanding of emotional intelligence can be incredibly beneficial for marketers engaged in sales, persuasion, and marketing efforts. By leveraging emotional intelligence skills such as empathy, effective communication, and emotional connection, marketers can build stronger relationships with their audience, drive more impactful marketing campaigns, and ultimately achieve greater success in their endeavors.

Miguel A. de Jesús is the Director of Business Development and Adjunct Professor at California State University (CSU) San Marcos, a Certified Professional Coach, Certified AI Consultant, and Emotional Intelligence Certified Coach. Miguel is also the bestselling author of several books, including *Let Your Emotional Intelligence Do the Talking: The 17 Skills Necessary for Performance Leadership with Your Boss, Family, Team, or Anyone Else Who Is Important to YOUR Transformational Life Goals* and *Success Leaves Clues: Tips and Techniques to Reach Your Maximum Potential*

Connect with Miguel on LinkedIn at https://www.linkedin.com/in/migueldj/

Chapter 8

What If You Embrace Marketing?

"Selling is the process of persuading a person that your product or service is of greater value to him than the price you're asking for it."

~ **Brian Tracy**

Embracing marketing and learning as much as you can about sales, persuasion, and more sets you apart from almost everyone else who is doing something even vaguely similar to what you are doing in your business.

I often think that if I had learned more about marketing in the decades before coming online, my entire life experience would have unfolded much differently. Allow me to elaborate on this...

In 1983 I became a real estate agent. Surrounded by people with many years of experience under their belt, I initiated conversations with them individually to find out how I could have better results and increase my sales.

One by one, each of these seasoned professionals disappointed me. When I led with the question "How do you like being in real estate sales?" they recoiled as if in pain, and then quickly changed the subject to something less objectionable and more palatable.

Soon, I learned to ask my questions differently, because I honestly wanted to know what they were thinking and experiencing in this field I was so excited to finally be a part of at that time.

The following week I was invited to caravan with the other agents. A caravan consists of several homes on the market for the first time, and sometimes a few that had been available at some point in the past and were now back on the market as a "relisting" to distinguish it from the others.

Someone in the office would create a list of the properties and a map, and hand out copies to everyone in the office who wanted to go.

It was so much fun to be included! Even though I was familiar with the area and could have easily driven in my own car, I instead opted to go with two or three other agents in one of their cars. My strategy was to make some new friends, listen to how they talked about real estate, and then later ask them individually what they liked most about real estate and their experiences in the business. Seemingly innocuous questions and a solid plan, I believed.

On that first Tuesday – our caravans were on Tuesdays and Fridays – we went into a gated area called Westchester County Estates. This area had opened that year – 1983 – and about half of the planned 104 single-family homes were either completed or in the process of being built.

Someone in the car mentioned that it was to be a "progressive lunch" today and I asked what that meant. The lady driving us dropped a flyer over her right shoulder and it fell into my lap in the back seat.

It turned out that there were eight homes for sale that we could preview that day. There was a map of the streets, and a diagram of which one to see first, then second, and so on. It took me a moment to figure it out, and when I did, I had to force myself not to laugh out loud. A "progressive" lunch meant that you would be served hors d'oeuvres at the first home, followed by soup and salad at the next house, and so on, ending with dessert and wine at the last home on the caravan.

Yes, it was shocking. No, I did not say a word. Yes, I ate something at every one of the eight homes we visited. No, I did not consume any alcohol, even though I was not driving and two different people asked me if I would drive their car back to the office so they could drink and ride back with someone else. I made an excuse about insurance coverage because this was years before I dared to speak up about anything by stating what I really thought to others.

My takeaways that day, and for months afterwards were related to the marketing of properties that needed to be sold for one reason or another. One thing was glaringly clear to me during those early days: If you presented a piece of property in the right way to the marketplace, it would sell more quickly and easily than a home that was a better value for the money, or one that was in a more desirable location or with superior amenities.

This knowledge took some time to percolate in my mind, and within six months I was one of my real estate office's top producers. And I'm proud to add that I never did anything that was even the least bit unethical, illegal, or just plain wrong, much to the chagrin of some of the people I met along the way.

Some would chide me for not being willing to slide into a "gray" area on command, but that was the time in my life when I finally decided everything was either black or white in my thinking, and that there was nothing in between.

I implore you to embrace marketing, and while you're at it, sales and persuasion as well. Your results will speak for themselves, and you will be able to serve people in a greater capacity than you ever would have imagined.

Chapter 9

The Lost Art of Persuasion with Ellen Finkelstein

"Every great presenter earns the respect of the audience (through her appearance, reputation, posture, voice, slides, introduction, etc.) and captures the attention of the audience by sending them love. The presenter who loves his audience the most, wins."

~ Seth Godin

This book would not be complete without the wisdom of Ellen Finkelstein. We first met at a marketing conference in Atlanta where we were both speakers and presenters on our more specific topics. Then we rediscovered each other in the online space and it wasn't long before we had become friends and colleagues.

We have co-authored two books, "Authors! The Quick Book to Business Method: Turning Your Book into an Ongoing Revenue Stream" and "Speakers! The Quick Public Speaking to Business Method: Turning Your Talk into an Ongoing Revenue Stream" and a third book is in the early stages of discussion and research for us. Ellen is a rare gem and you will benefit from what she is sharing with you here.

The Lost Art of Persuasion... Why Persuade?

Before you can be successful in persuading people, you need to know why you want to persuade them. If you aren't certain about that, you're not likely to succeed. Moreover, the more you consider your audience and what they need, the more effective you'll be.

You can only consistently succeed when you persuade someone to do something that's valuable to that person. This means that you know that your product or service will be useful for your potential customers. Perhaps your idea will be useful to senior management. That's the WHY

– you want to offer something valuable that will help them perform better in their job.

Techniques that mislead can work for only so long; eventually, they will catch up with you. In the 1970s and 1980s, the U.S. car companies banked on consumer loyalty and lots of advertising but eventually lost market share to Japanese car makers because their cars were inferior. (It's hard to gain back that trust later on, too!)

If you're pitching a product and realize that your potential customer or client doesn't need it, dare to say so. When you can do this, in situations where your customer does need the product, your integrity and certitude will come across. That's very powerful.

Therefore, the reason for persuading is to give. You have something useful to offer, whether it's a product, service, or idea. Instead of thinking about getting, think about giving. The best salespeople do this.

Think about a relationship between two people: let's say a husband and wife. If both focus on what they want to get out of the relationship, neither gives to the other. And guess what? If neither gives, neither gets! This can become a downward spiral. But if they both start to give, without concern for what they'll get, then they both receive maximum.

This principle is the lost art of persuasion. You focus on giving. I know it sounds silly, but you are like the blue fairy in Pinocchio who turns him into a real boy. You grant wishes. You fulfill desires. You help people grow, prosper, and succeed.

Pinocchio wished out loud to be a boy. But what if your potential client isn't as clear?

Know Your Audience

In any situation where you want to persuade, you need to find out the needs and desires of your audience. This is crucial, but what they want isn't always as obvious as it may seem. The information isn't always easy to get. Your audience might not know what they want, at least not consciously.

Perhaps you sell Customer Relationship Management (CRM) software. You know all of its benefits — better prospect tracking, more coordination among sales reps, great follow-up tools, and so on. So you pitch all of those benefits but don't get a positive response. It turns out that what the Sales Manager really wants is fewer sales reps coming to him complaining about computer hassles. They're asking, "How do I send an e-mail only to people who didn't reply to my offer of March 3rd?"

Or, "How do I get a list of everyone who bought the Pro version of our product between 1 and 2 years ago?"

Right now, the sales reps are all keeping their own records in Excel. You, as the salesperson, know that's a recipe for disaster, but they're doing a pretty good job and not losing much business — yet. So the Sales Manager's desire isn't obvious — unless you ask.

Many people, when they give a sales presentation, take time for questions, but they ask questions less often. They may feel that it's imposing on their prospective customer.

On the contrary, it's the greatest courtesy you can provide. You can say, "In order to offer you the product that best suits your needs, tell me what problems you're experiencing now. What worries you? What keeps you up at night?"

You can't grant a wish if you don't know what the wish is! The information isn't always easy to get. In a sales situation, you may not have advance direct contact with the decision maker. Senior management in your own company may not want to sit down with you to discuss their needs prior to your meeting to pitch an idea. So, sometimes, you need to do some research.

Similarly, if you're speaking on a webinar, you probably haven't been able to speak to the attendees in advance. Make the questions part of your presentation, as explained in the previous section.

Before you start, your audience might not be aware of their desires, so you need to elicit them. This is called turning latent desires into active desires. You do this by talking about the problem you can solve. Give an example or show a scenario. By clarifying the difficulty, you enable people to realize that they have this problem, even if they may not have thought about it before. Your examples and scenarios convert latent desires into active desires. They now have a wish and you can fulfill it.

Be open to adjusting your presentation to what the audience describes as their problem.

Qualifying an Audience

You probably don't want to sell to everyone. Getting the right audience in front of you is called "qualifying" an audience.

Qualifying an audience involves identifying the needs, desires, and pain points of your potential customers to determine if your product or service is a good fit for them. You also want to determine their ability and willingness to buy, if possible.

This can be done through research, surveys, and direct communication with your audience. The point is to do this before you invite them to a meeting so that you don't waste your time.

But why should you audience trust you?

Create a Rapport

Without trust, people won't let you persuade them. How do you establish trust? Here are some tips:

Don't be overly familiar with someone you don't know. Even "How are you?" can be seen as insincere with a stranger.

Never criticize either your audience or a competitor

Don't be evasive. Answer questions honestly. If you don't know, say so. If you offer to find the information and get back to the person, do so.

Don't make claims you can't back up or that are based on stretching statistics. If you're the "biggest" in your field, explain exactly what that means, so people can check the facts.

People feel more comfortable with someone who is like them. That's why salespeople always dress nicely whether calling on a potential customer in person or presenting online; it makes the customer feel more comfortable.

If your concern is to give, as I explained earlier, your audience feels your desire. Seth Godin wrote in his blog, "Every great presenter earns the respect of the audience (through her appearance, reputation, posture, voice, slides, introduction, etc.) and captures the attention of the audience by sending them love."

Godin concludes "The presenter who loves his audience the most, wins."

One valuable way to build trust is by presenting testimonials from previous customers. Or you can create case studies showing the results your customers have attained. Even a list of well-known customers is effective for building trust. People like to do what others are doing. If a respected company is your customer, others will want to be, too.

Email can also be a valuable tool for qualifying an audience and developing trust over time. By sending targeted and personalized emails to potential customers, you can gather information about their needs, desires, and pain points. This information can be used to tailor your sales pitch as well as show that you value your customers' opinions and are committed to meeting their needs.

Additionally, by sending regular emails with valuable content over time, you can establish yourself as a trusted source of information and build a positive relationship with your audience.

But how do you make your case?

Use the Persuasive Model

So many sales presentations start with an "About the Company" section. Have you attended a presentation like that? Wasn't it the most boring part? Didn't you want to get on with the important information? It's certainly not considerate to your audience to start by boring them. It's kinder to start by talking about their needs. Their needs are the problems they're facing — ones that you can solve. So, this is the most effective way to start. Presenting the problem is Step 1 of the Persuasive Model.

As I discussed earlier, you need to know what your audience wants. By stating and clarifying the problem, you focus your audience on what they need and open them up to your solution. In fact, it helps to elaborate on the effects of the problem:

Do they lack an effective follow-up to leads? Then they're losing business, market share, and profits.

Are they experiencing frequent technical problems? Then the delays are contributing to them losing business, market share, and profits.

Perhaps they don't have a coordinated method of purchasing software. Then they're spending too much and reducing their profits.

Step 2 is your solution, how you can solve the problem. You state your product, service, or idea as the solution to the problem. In our example, your Customer Relationship Management (CRM) software will help them gain business, increase market share, and expand profits. Your consulting will help them spend less and increase profits.

You've heard marketing experts say that you need to emphasize benefits. They say people buy benefits, not features. But benefits are not enough. Most people want to know why your specific solution provides the benefits they need and that's where features come in.

Telling isn't enough. They need to see. How do you show them? Use photos, graphs, data tables, and diagrams. If another company increased sales by 15%, show a simple graph. Use a clear and simple diagram to show how the software keeps track of contacts. Photos can be very powerful because people remember them clearly. These tools are the evidence that what you are saying is true.

As you explain what your product, service, or idea does, you tie it to the benefit, which is the result. In this way, you say that you can solve the problem, and how.

Step 3 is validation. Why is your solution better than others? Who else uses your solution? Why is your company the best provider? (Here's where your company history can go — at the end — as long as it's short.) Present testimonials, your guarantee, your experience, and your price to validate that you can provide the benefits you promise.

The benefits you offer, the features, and your ability to deliver are your unique selling proposition (USP). Your USP explains how you solve your prospect's problems and why you are the best one to do so.

But how do you keep it interesting?

Don't Be Boring!

Don't be boring! Boring your audience is not a gift. That 5-minute section on the history of your company (or worse, your industry) is boring, because your audience cares about their needs, not your company.

Bullets on slides are boring.

Full sentences on text-heavy slides are boring.

It's called Death by PowerPoint, but it isn't limited to your slides. Certainly, boring speeches existed long before PowerPoint!

There's a principle of copywriting called AIDA:

A: Attention –Start with an attention getter. Examples are a shocking statistic, a challenging question to the audience, a reference to today's news, or a surprising photo.

I: Interest – Get and keep the audience's interest by providing relevant information, using some appropriate humor, providing examples, and changing your approach. You might start with a straight talk, then move to a question-and-answer period, then do a demo. People don't want to sit through a straight lecture for more than 15 minutes, so be considerate of your audience.

D: Desire – Elicit desire by explaining results other customers got, displaying photos of satisfied customers, or describing how wonderful it is to work when the network isn't always crashing.

A: Action – Finally, elicit action by asking for the sale or suggesting the next step. You can spur on action with limited time discounts and other special offers. These techniques use the principle of scarcity to persuade people to act, yet at the same time they offer a real benefit, such as a lower price.

Summarize every few points. This helps organize the content for your audience. A teacher of mine called this the Oreo Cookie principle. It's similar to the old adage, "Tell 'em what you'll tell 'em. Tell 'em. Tell 'em what you told 'em," but you can summarize your point periodically as you go along. This technique helps your audience to better understand and remember what you're saying.

Stories and examples are wonderful ways to keep attention. They take the general and make it specific. People love to hear stories.

Jonah Lehrer, in his book, How We Decide, explains the importance and value of emotion in making decisions. In fact, neurological studies have shown that damage to certain areas of the brain important for emotion, seriously impair the ability to make decisions.

But how do you make your point clear?

Be Clear!

Purposeful obfuscation is unethical and self-defeating. Most presenters don't try to confuse but don't consider whether their audience can understand what they're saying. When you know your audience, you can adjust your message to their needs. Don't be overly technical for a non-technical audience; don't be overly simplistic for a technical audience. Don't dump information that's not needed on them, just because you have it. Every word on a slide and every item on a chart should have a purpose for making your point.

An overview or executive summary helps the audience know where you're going. By organizing the content for them in advance, you can help them follow you more easily.

Use clear logic. If you're not sure, ask an uninvolved colleague or friend to hear you out. Ask if your talk makes logical sense. Text, charts, tables, and diagrams need to be clear. Find ways to communicate with images, charts, and diagrams. Don't rely solely on words. Both learning theory and brain research conclude that people can't effectively read (text on a slide) and listen (to what you're saying) at the same time. So why are you reading your slides? Put fewer words on your slides and use notes.

Finally, after the question-and-answer period, end with a clear conclusion that ties up your points and leads your audience to action.

But what if your audience objects?

Handle Objections as Opportunities

In order to persuade, you need to overcome objections. This process is the nitty-gritty of persuasion. Brainstorm possible objections in advance and have your answers ready.

Robert Cialdini, in his classic book, Influence: The Psychology of Persuasion, lists six principles of persuasion and more recently added a seventh:

1. **Scarcity:** If what you're offering is unique and rare, people want more of it. People want to know what they will lose if they don't buy, or agree with you.
2. **Authority:** People want to follow experts, but you need to be both knowledgeable and truthful. Admitting weakness actually helps you gain credibility.
3. **Consensus (social proof):** People follow others. Testimonials and referrals are very valuable. When a potential customer raises objections, it can mean that you didn't successfully unravel the customer's needs. Accept the objections, and clarify them. You can do this by feeding back the statement for confirmation. "So you're saying that what you really need is someone to call and help you through a networking crisis?" Use objections to get back to your audience's needs. Explain how you can alleviate the customer's concern.
4. **(Sympathy) Liking:** People like those who are like them and are more likely to say yes to those they like. They respond best to someone who likes them.
5. **Reciprocity:** If you do someone a favor, that person feels obligated to return it. Remember that your job is to help your audience.
6. **Commitment and consistency:** When potential customers write down a commitment, they're more likely to live up to it. They want to be consistent with their past actions and beliefs.

7. **Unity:** When your audience feels part of a group/community, they allow themselves to be influenced by that group.

But how do you close?

Close with Action Steps

When you've finished your presentation, answered questions, and provided a summary, it's time to suggest action. "I suggest that the next step is..."

Remind them of the benefits and confirm that the solution you laid out is what they need, based on the needs they have expressed. Confirm that they'll get the benefits, "This course will really change your business around so that you can finally move ahead and achieve your goal to make 6 figures in the coming year," for example.

Finally, remind your audience of others who have had success with your course (or product, service, or idea). "So-and-so just made 6 figures for the first time!" Then again suggest the next step.

But what's the goal of all this?

Help the World Grow

Maybe you think of your job as just a job. Don't! Find a purpose! Whether you're selling a product, service, or idea, if it's worthwhile, you're helping people. In their book, The One Minute Millionaire, Mark Victor Hansen and Robert G. Allen say, "The Enlightened Millionaire enjoys creating wealth that improves the lives of many people. The goal is to enrich oneself while enriching others." That enrichment isn't only financial.

As the authors note, "Almost anyone can become a millionaire, but we're hoping you'll aim for enlightenment at the same time." So, use your persuasive skills in a win-win situation, to help both you and your audience. By focusing mostly on helping your audience, maximum results will come back to you.

The principle is: You have to give to receive.

Connecting with Ellen Finkelstein

Ellen is a recognized expert, speaker, trainer, and best-selling author on PowerPoint, presentation skills, and speaking. Her articles have appeared in numerous magazines, newsletters, and blogs.

Ellen Finkelstein is also a PowerPoint MVP (Most Valuable Professional), a Microsoft award for experts in its product who contribute to the user community, one of only 18 in the United States.

Her website offers a huge assortment of tips, techniques, tutorials, and articles on these topics.

She also teaches speakers, writers, and experts to get their knowledge out to the world with a knowledge-based online business at ChangetheWorldMarketing.com.

SECTION THREE

WHAT IF YOU LEARN AND IMPLEMENT MARKETING AND SALES STRATEGIES?

"Everything we do in our lives is preparing us for something that will arise in the future, even though we don't yet know what that will be."

~ Connie Ragen Green

Think back to a time when you were in school and learning about a topic that was important to you. Perhaps you were in high school and studying biology, and this inspired you to want to go to medical school and become a doctor or researcher. Maybe you were in college and the study of the great philosophers sparked your interest to the point that you decided to go to graduate school to devote your life to this topic.

If you can relate to this in any way, what was the outcome? Did you follow through and complete whatever coursework, internship, or something else that was necessary for you to achieve your dream and goal? Or, did you let it go and make up the reasons – excuses – for why you took a different path?

In my life, I passed up every opportunity that was in front of me and made up elaborate and detailed stories as to why I could not reach, or even attempt to go after my dream. These excuses held me back and kept me safely inside the bubble of my comfort zone.

That changed in 1986, when something occurred that motivated me to change my life completely, no matter what it would take for me to achieve my goal.

When the Challenger Space Shuttle disaster occurred on January 8th, 1986, I was one of millions of people who was deeply affected by this tragedy. Overnight, people signed up for the armed services, joined groups of volunteers in a variety of areas, became police officers, and more. I was part of the "and more" group who became a classroom teacher.

I had to take out a government loan to go back to college to earn my teaching credential and make my transition into this new world. Los Angeles was one of many cities throughout North America that was experiencing a teacher shortage during the 1980s. I was offered something called an Emergency Credential and assigned to a classroom of 5th and 6th graders. I wrote about this in an earlier chapter, but this is more of a personal story.

Teaching was my calling. I loved every moment in the classroom. Eager young minds were ready to soak up everything I could give them. I had the freedom back then to add my own interests and experiences to my daily lesson plans. I'm a philatelist, so I brought in commemorative stamps and lessons prepared by the US Postal Service. I was just getting interested in computers and technology, so I brought in one of my computers from home and successfully wrote and received a Grant that provided three more for my classroom. These were Apple IIe desktop models, if you remember the early computers. This was before color monitors and back when a mouse was still a small rodent.

Time passed. Life happened. I had cancer for the first time and had to take a leave of absence from teaching. I survived and needed work, so I did some commercial appraisal assignments for someone I knew.

Soon, I returned to the classroom; a 6th grade class at a new school. It was in January, and the kids were cold and unresponsive to me. One day a boy named Omar said, "So how long are you gonna stay?" and this caught me by surprise.

I dug deeper. The teacher I was replacing had retired when they went on break in December and didn't mention to his class that he wouldn't be returning. A series of substitutes had come through the revolving door until they hired me. I knew better than to demand their respect. Instead, I set out to earn their trust, day by day, interaction by interaction. I was up to this challenge and looked forward to arriving early each morning at my new school.

These children were not as tough as they wanted to appear. On the outside they wore a crusty shell; on the inside, they were sweet and kind and frightened and vulnerable. They had been to Hell and back on many occasions already. We were in an area controlled by two rival gangs and they had experienced violence firsthand.

I asked them to share their stories with me... orally, handwritten, and typed with two fingers on the computers in our classroom. I cried as I read and listened to what they were willing to share. And over the next couple of months, I fell in love with these children and their families.

The reason I am telling you this story is to impress upon you the importance of following through with your goals and dreams. If I hadn't been deeply moved by seeing the high school students on television as they watched the Space Shuttle launch and then explode in front of their eyes, I wouldn't have moved heaven and earth to become a teacher to follow in Christa McAuliffe's footsteps.

Are you inspired and motivated by me, or by one of the people I asked to contribute to this book? Do you want to change your life and that of the people close to you by creating a business based on sales, persuasion, and marketing? If so, then you are in for the ride of your life.

My quote at the beginning of this section says it all...

> *"Everything we do in our lives is preparing us for something that will arise in the future, even though we don't yet know what that will be."*

When I attended a seminar in Los Angeles years ago and met a woman who had created an online course that was also in a physical format with a book and two CDs, I was inspired to do something similar. Allow your dreams and goals to wash over you each day. Daydream the possibilities and imagine your life on your terms. I believe in you!

Chapter 10

The Psychology of Persuading the Pants Off Them

"Master the topic, the message, and the delivery."

~ **Steve Jobs**

Once you learn about the psychology necessary to become an effective marketer and use it ethically in your daily life, everything will change for you. Even without knowing you personally, I can tell you that you are most likely an expert in this area already.

The World Will Be Your Oyster

Young children are masterful when it comes to the psychology of persuasion. Once they persuade their subjects, they go into full marketing mode to close the deal. It's the one-two punch that seldom fails to deliver the desired result.

Imagine a child of eight or nine years of age who wants a bicycle. They've recently experienced another child with a bike and now it's all they can think about from morning to night each day. Let's call this child Abigail for the example I'm describing here.

Abigail spent a few days last week with her cousins, and one of them, Billy had just received a shiny new bike for his birthday. He was learning to ride it, and while Abigail was at their house his parents were able to remove the training wheels.

As Billy flew down the sidewalk and circled through their cul-de-sac Abigail decided, unconsciously that she wanted to have the same experience.

Upon returning home, she expressed this newfound desire to her parents during dinner. It was met with a barrage of reasons why she would not be receiving a bicycle of her own any time soon. Her mother and father took turns bursting her bubble and setting her straight:

"Do you have any idea how much a new bicycle would cost?"

"Bicycles are dangerous. You could fall and break your arm, or worse."

"Aunt Stephanie and Uncle Bill spoil their kids. We don't believe in that style of parenting."

"You already have roller skates. Why do you need a bike?"

Abigail was getting whiplash from looking back and forth at her parents while they took turns telling her no but with explanations.

Being the very smart and polite young lady her parents were used to, Abigail thought carefully before she spoke. One wrong move and she might be in high school before she got a bike. But with a little psychology in the beginning, she'd be able to open the door to discussing this further in the very near future.

She took one more bite of her vegetables before continuing.

"Billy did fall down once while he was practicing in the backyard. But he was on the lawn and had his jeans on so he didn't even get scraped up. And then when Uncle Bill was running along beside him in the cul-de-sac, he held his arms out so he could have caught Billy if he fell."

On that note, the conversation ended and tapioca pudding was served for dessert. Abigail had won the first round of this discussion, and she knew it.

Let's unpack what happened here. Abigail realized immediately that she had broached a controversial topic with her parents. From the statements they made, she concluded that they were most concerned with her safety, so that is what she focused on in her reply. Mom and Dad probably hadn't thought about her being able to practice in the backyard. Right away, she had introduced a plausible alternative to riding on the sidewalk or in the street. And having her parents run alongside her would make it possible for them to come to her rescue if she did start to fall.

As she licked the spoon from the last bit of pudding and took her bowl into the kitchen to help with the dishes before being asked, Abigail planned her next move in her quest to get a bicycle of her own.

If you're following my line of reasoning here, you know that Abigail must next conquer the issue of the bicycle being expensive.

Even though she is still a little girl, she understands that money doesn't grow on trees. But Abigail hasn't bought into this lack mentality and still believes that everything is possible.

After thinking about it for a full day, she brings up the topic with her father while they are driving to the dry cleaners to pick up some clothes and a bedspread that are ready.

"Daddy, do you remember the check for ten dollars that Grandma gave me for having a good report card?"

"Yes, of course. We went to the bank together to cash it. You still have that money in your piggy bank, don't you?"

"Yes. And I also have my birthday money and most of my allowance from the past two months."

"Good girl. It's important to save for a rainy day."

Abigail doesn't immediately respond, as this "rainy day" concept could be a tricky one.

"I know. But I remember the story you told Aunt Stephanie and Uncle Bill when they said they wanted to buy a house but were afraid to use their savings."

Dad is quiet for a moment because he has a sneaking suspicion that he is about to be talked into something.

"Yes. Go on, Abigail."

"Well, if someone saves up for something they really want, and if that thing is also something that will make them happy, they kind of have to use their savings to buy it or there's no point in saving. Isn't that right, Daddy?"

He sits up straighter in his seat and turns off the radio.

"Tell me more, Abby."

Abigail has to restrain herself from showing her delight. When her father calls her Abby, she knows he's on her side. She pauses before continuing.

"I opened my piggy bank and counted all of my money before I went to bed last night. I think after eight more allowances and one more birthday, I might have enough for a bicycle like Billy's, but gold instead of blue and with lower handlebars. Billy has high handlebars and those might not be as safe."

Bam! This one-two punch covered cost and safety in three sentences.

Dad was silent as they drove on to the cleaners, and that spoke volumes.

The final hurdle to cross was the issue of her cousin Billy being spoiled. He wasn't or at least she didn't think so, and Aunt Stephanie and Uncle Bill seemed like really good parents, at least in her experience with them over the years.

Abigail called Billy on the weekend to see what he was doing.

"Hi, Billy. Watcha doin'?"

"Nothing."

Something was wrong. He wasn't being forthcoming or even making his usual wisecracks, so she would have to dig a little.

"Did you go to your friend's birthday party? I can't remember his name."

"No."

"But I thought they were doing something at the party you were excited about. Weren't they going to have a clown? No, it was a magician. You love magicians."

"I got in trouble at school for making fun of a girl. And then I failed my spelling test. I'm grounded for a week."

Abigail spent the next five minutes asking him the details and attempting to make Billy feel a little better. She ended the call by reminding him that it was her mom's birthday in two weeks and that she would see him then.

Gazing out the kitchen window for a few more minutes, she practiced the words a few times before speaking with her mother.

At her mom's birthday party exactly two weeks later, her parents surprised Abigail and everyone else by presenting her with a shiny new bike. It was exactly as she had described it, and even came with a matching gold helmet, wrist pads, and knee pads.

Can you figure out what happened to bring this about? Okay, I'll tell you exactly what happened...

After speaking on the phone with Billy two weeks earlier, Abigail brought up the incident at dinner that evening. She shared every detail and focused on the parts where Billy had made mistakes by making fun of someone and then not apologizing, and choosing to not study his spelling words before the test.

She emphasized in great detail what Billy could have done instead, and how she was lucky to have parents who helped her figure out what not to do and how to fix things when they go wrong.

Then she talked about how strict Aunt Stephanie and Uncle Bill had been with Billy and that she didn't know that about them. She recalled the moment when her parents glanced across the table at each other, and the look told Abigail they had made a mistake in thinking Billy was spoiled.

I'd love to tell you this is a true story from my childhood, but that is not the case. Instead, it's a story I have carefully crafted over the years as an example of how the use of psychology is so important in our lives. And I don't ever think of this strategy as being tricky or based on lies. Instead, I believe that persuading someone to do something that you know for a fact, based on your experience and expertise in that area will bring about a positive outcome for them is the right thing to do. I did this most recently when I was recommending a colleague's new membership site that included personal help with creating journals, planners, and other printables as a business that could be run from home, or from anywhere in the world with only an internet connection required.

The Role of Psychology in Both Online and In-Person Marketing

Psychology plays a crucial role in effective marketing, influencing consumer behavior and decision-making. Whether in the online or brick-and-mortar realm, understanding psychological principles can help marketers create more compelling messages, build stronger connections with customers, and ultimately drive profitability. Here are some ways psychology comes into play:

Marketing: Understanding Consumer Behavior

Analyzing online consumer behavior, such as click-through rates, time spent on pages, and online interactions, helps marketers tailor their strategies to meet the preferences of their audience.

In physical stores, observing and understanding how customers move through the space, what catches their attention, and how they interact with products can inform merchandising and layout decisions.

Creating Persuasive Messaging with Marketing

Crafting persuasive copy that appeals to emotions, addresses pain points, and provides solutions is crucial. Techniques like storytelling and the use of influential language can be highly effective.

In physical stores, signage, product displays, and in-store communication should be designed to influence customer perceptions and decisions.

Utilizing Social Proof in Marketing

Customer reviews, testimonials, and social media interactions act as powerful social proof. Positive endorsements from others influence online shoppers.

Seeing a busy store or witnessing others making purchases creates a sense of social proof that can attract more customers.

Creating a Sense of Urgency

Limited-time offers, countdowns, and exclusive online deals create a sense of urgency, tapping into the psychological principle of scarcity.

Brick-and-Mortar: In-store promotions with expiration dates or limited stock can encourage quicker decision-making.

Building Brand Loyalty

Consistent branding, engaging content, and personalized experiences online contribute to building a strong brand that customers feel loyal to.

Brick-and-Mortar: Exceptional in-store experiences, quality products, and outstanding customer service contribute to brand loyalty in physical businesses.

Cognitive Biases and Decision-Making

Understanding cognitive biases, such as anchoring, confirmation bias, and loss aversion, can help marketers present information in a way that aligns with how people naturally think and make decisions.

Brick-and-Mortar: Price anchoring, for example, can be used in physical stores by showcasing a higher-priced item first, making subsequent items seem like a better deal.

Personalization and Segmentation

Personalizing online experiences based on user behavior, preferences, and demographics enhances engagement and increases the likelihood of conversion.

Brick-and-Mortar: Loyalty programs, targeted promotions, and personalized customer interactions in physical stores contribute to a more personalized customer experience.

Visual Appeal and Aesthetics

Visual elements, color psychology, and website design influence how users perceive a brand and its products.

Brick-and-Mortar: In physical stores, the aesthetics of the space, including layout, lighting, and product displays, impact the overall customer experience.

Fear of Missing Out (FOMO)

Highlighting exclusive online offers, limited-time discounts, or unique online events can trigger the fear of missing out and drive online sales.

Brick-and-Mortar: Limited-time in-store promotions and events can create a similar sense of urgency.

By integrating these psychological principles into marketing strategies, both online and in physical businesses, marketers can connect with their audience on a deeper level, influence decision-making, and create more effective and profitable campaigns.

Sales, Persuasion, and Marketing

Here are some key insights and advice for a newer marketer looking to leverage persuasion to make sales:

Understand the Principles of Influence

Familiarize yourself with the six principles of influence that are outlined in Robert Cialdini's book "Influence: The Psychology of Persuasion." These principles are reciprocity, commitment, social proof, authority, liking, and scarcity. Knowing how these principles work will give you a solid foundation for effective persuasion in marketing.

Build Rapport and Likability

People are more likely to buy from those they like and trust. Building rapport and likability is crucial in marketing. Connect with your audience on a personal level, show genuine interest, and find common ground. This can be achieved through storytelling, relatable content, and authentic communication.

Utilize Social Proof

Leverage the power of social proof to influence potential customers. Highlight testimonials, reviews, and case studies that showcase positive experiences from previous customers. People are more likely to trust a product or service that others have found valuable.

Establish Authority

Position yourself and your brand as experts in your field. Share your knowledge through blogs, articles, and other content that demonstrates your expertise. Authority is a powerful influencer, and people are more likely to follow the recommendations of those they perceive as knowledgeable.

Create a Sense of Scarcity

The principle of scarcity suggests that people are more motivated by the thought of losing something than gaining it. Create a sense of urgency or exclusivity in your marketing messages. Limited-time offers, exclusive deals, or product scarcity can drive people to make decisions faster.

Employ the Power of Reciprocity

Offer something of value upfront to create a sense of obligation. This could be in the form of free content, samples, or exclusive access. When people feel that they have received something valuable, they are more likely to reciprocate by making a purchase.

Use Persuasive Storytelling

Craft compelling stories that resonate with your audience. Humans are wired to respond to narratives, and storytelling can be a powerful marketing tool. Stories create emotional connections and make your messages more memorable.

Incorporate Pre-Suasion Techniques

Building on the concepts from Cialdini's book "Pre-Suasion: A Revolutionary Way to Influence and Persuade," consider the importance of setting the stage for persuasion. Before presenting your main message, create a context or frame that primes your audience to be more receptive to your ideas.

And remember that the art of persuasion is a positive concept. We have all been gently persuaded to do things we initially did not want any part of, and later discovered that we didn't want to live without.

Test and Iterate

Marketing is an evolving field, and what works today may not work tomorrow. Test different strategies, messages, and approaches to see what resonates best with your audience. Use data and analytics to measure the effectiveness of your campaigns and be ready to adapt based on the results.

Remember, the key to successful persuasion in marketing is to understand human psychology, build trust, and create meaningful connections with your audience. By incorporating these principles, you can enhance your ability to influence and make more effective sales.

Ensuring that your strategies for sales, marketing, persuasion, and influence are not perceived as purely self-serving is crucial for building trust and credibility. Here are some strategies to achieve that:

Focus on Customer Value

Shift the emphasis of your messaging from the benefits to your company to the value it provides to customers. Clearly communicate how your product or service solves their problems, meets their needs, or enhances their lives. This customer-centric approach demonstrates that you prioritize their interests.

The people in my online community consist of prospects, subscribers, customers, and clients. I consider everyone to be a blessing in my life and my primary focus and goal is around how I may best serve them.

Transparent Communication

Be open and transparent in your communication. Clearly articulate your offerings, pricing, and any terms and conditions. Transparency builds trust, and customers are more likely to engage with businesses that are upfront about what they offer.

Entertain, Educate, and Inform

I learned early on that marketing included entertaining your prospects and clients with a strategy referred to as edutainment. After all these years, I lead with entertainment in my marketing. Position yourself as an industry expert by providing valuable information and education to your audience. Share insights, tips, and relevant content that genuinely help your audience, even if it doesn't directly lead to a sale. By demonstrating your expertise and commitment to helping, you build trust and credibility.

Authenticity in Branding

Be authentic in your brand representation. Share the human side of your company, including your values, culture, and the people behind the brand. Authenticity fosters a sense of connection, and customers are more likely to engage with businesses that align with their values.

Customer Testimonials and Case Studies

Let your satisfied customers speak for you. Share genuine testimonials and case studies that highlight positive experiences with your product or service. This social proof adds credibility and demonstrates real-world benefits.

I also create and share my own case studies with my prospects and clients. Most recently I shared how I am marketing a book I co-authored with my awesome friend and colleague Ellen Finkelstein, "Speakers! The Quick Public Speaking to Business Method: Turning Your Talk into an Ongoing Revenue Stream".

Before writing the book, I created an eCourse on How to Become a Public Speaker that is delivered through autoresponder messages.

Then I wrote a blog post about the fear people sometimes have around public speaking.

The goal is to sell more books, teach people more about public speaking as a business strategy and income stream, and also to grow my email list in the process. Everything here: the book, the blog post, and the eCourse work in unison to help me to achieve my goals.

Long-Term Relationships Over Quick Wins

Prioritize building long-term relationships with customers rather than focusing solely on short-term gains. Show commitment to customer satisfaction, post-purchase support, and ongoing engagement. This approach helps establish trust and encourages repeat business.

Community Engagement

Engage with your community, both online and offline. Participate in relevant discussions, address customer concerns, and actively listen to feedback. By being part of a larger community, you demonstrate a commitment to mutual benefit beyond immediate transactions. I have been a part of Rotary, an international service organization since coming online in 2006, and this group was the springboard for me to connect with other non-profit groups in both of the cities I call home.

Spending time with the people I have met through these organizations has broadened my horizons and enabled me to see the world from different perspectives, both literally and by traveling to locations all around our planet.

Sustainability and Social Responsibility

Integrate sustainability and social responsibility into your business practices. Communicate your commitment to ethical business conduct, environmental stewardship, and social causes. Consumers are increasingly valuing businesses that contribute positively to society.

Balanced Self-Promotion

While it's essential to promote your products or services, balance your self-promotion with valuable content that goes beyond sales pitches. Share industry insights, tips, and relevant information that your audience finds genuinely useful.

Ask for Feedback and Listen

Actively seek feedback from your customers and listen to their concerns and suggestions. Demonstrating a willingness to improve based on customer input reinforces that your business is focused on meeting their needs.

By incorporating these strategies, you can help ensure that your sales, marketing, persuasion, and influence efforts are perceived as genuine and customer-focused rather than solely self-serving. Building trust takes time, but the long-term benefits of customer loyalty and positive brand perception are well worth the effort.

Robert Cialdini's books, "Influence: The Psychology of Persuasion" and "Pre-Suasion: A Revolutionary Way to Influence and Persuade," contain many impactful quotes. Here are a couple of quotes that can make a difference for entrepreneurs, salespeople, and those just getting started with marketing:

From "Influence: The Psychology of Persuasion":

"The way to love anything is to realize that it might be lost."

~ G.K. Chesterton

This quote emphasizes the principle of scarcity and the psychological impact of perceived loss. In marketing, creating a sense of scarcity or limited availability can enhance the desirability of a product or service.

From "Pre-Suasion: A Revolutionary Way to Influence and Persuade":

"The best way to believe in the future is to create it."

~ Abraham Lincoln

This quote underscores the power of priming and setting the stage for persuasion. In marketing, understanding the concept of pre-suasion and strategically influencing the mindset of your audience before presenting your main message can be a game-changer.

Remember, the insights from these quotes reflect the psychological principles that can be harnessed to create effective marketing strategies. Whether it's by tapping into the fear of loss or by proactively shaping perceptions, these concepts can guide entrepreneurs and salespeople in their efforts to influence and persuade.

When you implement even some of the strategies I'm sharing here, as well as those shared by marketing giants from the beginning of time, your thoughts and focus will begin to shift dramatically.

Connecting and Building Relationships with Thought Leaders

Marlon Sanders is someone I connected with early on, and over the years we have co-authored books with Joe Vitale and several other marketers. Along with Miguel A. de Jesús, Ellen Finkelstein, and Carl Galletti, experts and thought leaders who contributed chapters for this book, Marlon Sanders is an awesome human being I am proud to call my friend.

He is recognized as a marketing expert, particularly in the realm of Internet marketing. However, specific details about his current strategies or approaches to marketing and sales of digital products may have evolved since then. To gain the most accurate and up-to-date information, I recommend checking Marlon Sanders' official website, blog, or recent publications.

That being said, based on his past teachings and approaches, Marlon is known for emphasizing certain principles in online marketing:

Focus on Value Proposition

Marlon often stresses the importance of clearly communicating the value of a digital product. This involves understanding the needs and desires of the target audience and positioning the product as a solution to their problems or a means to fulfill their desires.

Effective Copywriting

Copywriting is a crucial aspect of online marketing, and Sanders has provided insights into creating persuasive and compelling copy.

Crafting headlines, messages, and calls to action (CTAs) that resonate with the audience and address their pain points is key.

Building a Relationship with the Audience

Marlon also emphasizes the significance of building relationships with your audience. This involves regular communication through various channels, such as email marketing, to establish trust and credibility. Building a connection with the audience can lead to increased loyalty and repeat business.

Automation and Systems

He often advocates for the use of automation and systems in marketing. This includes setting up sales funnels, email sequences, and other automated processes to streamline the marketing and sales process.

Testing and Optimization

A key aspect of Marlon Sanders' approach involves testing different elements of a marketing campaign and optimizing based on the results. This includes testing different headlines, offers, and strategies to identify what resonates best with the target audience. I continue to be in awe of how he creates and then tests his marketing campaigns, and does not settle for results that are less than stellar.

Product Launch Strategies

Marlon has shared insights into effective product launch strategies. This may involve creating anticipation before the launch, offering special promotions or bonuses, and utilizing scarcity or limited-time offers to drive sales.

I'm able to speak with him on the phone when we both have the time, and I continue to be amazed at how he thinks and looks at things from his expert perspective.

Education and Training

Marlon has been known to provide educational resources and training programs to help marketers and entrepreneurs improve their skills. This may include courses, webinars, and other materials focused on various aspects of online marketing.

I hope you are aware of how special it is to learn from experts and thought leaders in areas you wish to master. Without Marlon Sanders and others in my life, my business would be nowhere close to where it is now and what I am able to achieve as a result.

Chapter 11

Recurring and Passive Income

"Compound interest is the eighth wonder of the world. He who understands it, earns it. He who doesn't, pays it."

~ Albert Einstein

The thought of creating recurring income streams entices many people to join the ranks of online entrepreneurs all over the world who are doing this in a seemingly effortless manner. While this business model isn't exactly like what Einstein supposedly said about compound interest, it comes very close.

Membership sites come to mind first, but there are hundreds of ways to serve people so they are excited to pay you by the month or annually for what you provide. This business model introduced me to the concept of earning income while you sleep, or are engaged with other activities that you love so it will never feel like you're working at a job.

Sell It Once… Get Paid Over and Over Again

Long ago, I had my first show business friend. She was a woman who lived down the street from me, and we met because our dogs had become friends while we were out walking them.

One day I asked her what kind of work she did and that's when she told me that she was an actress. She quickly clarified that for me by saying that she was in television commercials, but that didn't make a difference to me.

I was intrigued and over the next several months she told me stories about her agent, going on auditions, filming the commercials, and getting paid. She earned money when she finished filming, but that was only the tip of the iceberg.

She explained to me that once the commercial was finished and aired on television, she received something called residuals every time the commercial aired. She even showed me a check she had received for a commercial she had been in over five years earlier. The check was for just over a hundred dollars, but the bigger picture was that she had done nothing additional to be able to continue earning income. That idea of residuals stuck in my mind, but I had no plans to become an actress and act in commercials.

Little did I know that decades later I would start an online business that would operate on the same principle of working once and being paid over and over again for years to come. That's exactly how it works when you create a product or a course that's delivered virtually. Once you put everything in place, you've created an asset you may sell.

Moving the Free Line

I first heard the phrase "moving the free line" as a new online entrepreneur and marketer in 2006.

Moving the Free Line

Does moving the free line refer to giving away more or less for free to your prospects?

"Moving the free line" refers to the strategic decision to offer more valuable content, products, or services for free to your prospects and audience. It means being generous with the value you provide upfront without immediate monetary exchange. By moving the free line, you aim to attract and engage your audience, build trust, and create a stronger relationship with potential customers.

This strategy is based on the idea that providing substantial value for free can lead to various benefits, such as increased brand loyalty, word-of-mouth marketing, enhanced customer trust, and more effective lead generation. While it might seem counterintuitive to give away a lot for free, it can ultimately lead to a more successful and profitable business in the long run by creating a solid foundation of trust and goodwill with your audience.

The free line is what you use to illustrate how much value is in the products and services you give away for free to your audience and prospective clients. It also helps you decide how much you can charge for your products and services.

What you're trying to do is give your prospective clients some of the value you offer with your products and services upfront for nothing. This sort of activity gives your clients a much clearer idea of what it is you offer, and how good you are at doing what you do. It also holds you to a higher standard when you deliver your products and services too, which is a nice bonus.

"Moving the Free Line" is a marketing strategy that emphasizes the strategic use of free content, products, or services to attract and engage potential customers. The goal is to provide value to your audience and build trust, ultimately leading to a stronger customer relationship and increased revenue. Here's a more detailed explanation of this concept and how it can benefit new marketers and online entrepreneurs:

- ☞ Attracting and Engaging Prospects: Offering valuable content or services for free is a way to attract and engage your target audience. By providing something of value without an immediate monetary exchange, you can create interest and draw people into your marketing funnel. This approach can be particularly effective in today's online landscape, where consumers expect to find free information and resources.
- ☞ Building Trust and Credibility: Moving the free line allows you to demonstrate your expertise and build trust with your audience. When you consistently deliver high-quality free content or services, it establishes your credibility and positions you as an authority in your industry. This trust is crucial for converting prospects into paying customers in the long run.
- ☞ Showcasing Value: The concept of the free line also involves showcasing the value of your products and services. When you offer a taste of what you provide for free, it helps potential customers understand the benefits and quality of what you offer. This transparency can make them more willing to invest in your paid offerings.

- ☞ Lead Generation: Free content and services can serve as a powerful lead generation tool. By offering something valuable for free, you can collect contact information, such as email addresses, from interested individuals. This allows you to nurture these leads over time, gradually guiding them toward becoming paying customers.
- ☞ Pricing Strategy: Moving the free line can help you determine how much to charge for your products and services. When you provide a free version or sample, you can assess how well it resonates with your audience and gather feedback. This data can inform your pricing strategy, ensuring that you set prices that align with the perceived value you offer.
- ☞ Higher Standards and Accountability: When you provide free content or services, it creates a commitment to delivering high-quality offerings. Knowing that potential customers have experienced your free content and are judging your quality, you're incentivized to maintain high standards in your products and services. This accountability can lead to better customer satisfaction and loyalty.
- ☞ Upsell Opportunities: Offering free content or products can also create opportunities for upselling. Once someone has benefited from your free offerings and values what you provide, they may be more inclined to explore your paid products or services, which offer even more value or features.
- ☞ Word of Mouth and Referrals: A successful free line strategy can lead to positive word-of-mouth marketing and referrals. Satisfied customers and engaged audience members are more likely to recommend your business to others, helping you expand your reach and acquire new customers organically.

In summary, moving the free line is a strategic approach that uses free offerings to attract, engage, and build trust with your target audience. It provides numerous benefits, including demonstrating your expertise, generating leads, influencing your pricing strategy, and holding you to high standards. This strategy can be a valuable tool for new marketers and online entrepreneurs looking to establish their presence and grow their businesses in a competitive digital landscape.

This doesn't mean you should give too much away to prospects and potential clients and customers. How much free stuff is too much?

The amount of free content or value you should provide to prospects, potential clients, and customers can vary based on your business goals, industry, and specific circumstances. It's essential to strike a balance between offering value for free and monetizing your products or services effectively. Here are some considerations to help you determine how much is too much:

☞ Align with Your Business Model: Your business model and revenue strategy should guide how much free content or value you offer. For example, a subscription-based model may offer limited free content to attract subscribers, while a freemium model provides a basic version for free and charges for premium features.

☞ Value vs. Cost: Evaluate the value of your free offerings versus the cost of providing them. If the cost of delivering free content or services is too high, it might not be sustainable in the long run.

☞ Audience Expectations: Consider industry norms and what your target audience expects. In some industries, providing a lot of free content is common and necessary for audience engagement. In others, offering less free content may be more appropriate.

☞ Competitive Landscape: Analyze what your competitors are doing. Your approach to free offerings should be competitive but also unique and tailored to your brand's strengths.

☞ Lead Generation: If your primary goal is lead generation, offering valuable free content can be more extensive. However, it's crucial to balance this with effective lead nurturing strategies to convert those leads into paying customers.

☞ Quality over Quantity: Focus on the quality of your free offerings rather than the quantity. Providing a few highly valuable resources or services can be more effective than overwhelming your audience with a large volume of mediocre content.

- ☞ Monetization Points: Identify key monetization points within your sales funnel. You may offer a lot of free content early in the funnel to attract prospects and gradually reduce the amount as you move toward paid offerings.
- ☞ Feedback and Data: Continuously gather feedback and data to assess the impact of your free offerings. Monitor conversion rates, engagement, and customer feedback to adjust your strategy as needed.
- ☞ Testing and Optimization: Consider A/B testing and experimentation to find the right balance. Test different levels of free content and measure the impact on conversions and revenue.
- ☞ Long-Term Value: Keep in mind the long-term value of a customer. Providing a lot of value for free can be justified if it leads to loyal, long-term customers who make significant purchases over time.

You can see that there isn't a one-size-fits-all answer to how much free content is too much. Your strategy should be tailored to your business objectives and your audience's preferences. It's important to find the right balance that allows you to attract, engage, and convert prospects while ensuring the sustainability and profitability of your business. Regular assessment, optimization, and flexibility in your approach are key to finding the optimal balance for your specific situation.

How do you know what is the best thing to give away to your prospects as you are building and growing your online business early on? I'm thinking of short reports, checklists, and templates related to my products, courses, and coaching programs.

When you're building and growing your online business, offering valuable free content is a powerful way to attract and engage prospects. The type of content you give away should align with your brand, expertise, and the needs of your target audience. Short reports, checklists, and templates are excellent choices, and they can be highly effective. Here's why:

☞ Short Reports: Short reports are valuable because they can provide in-depth insights, solve specific problems, or offer expert advice on a particular topic related to your products or services. They can showcase your expertise and serve as a sample of the quality your audience can expect from your paid offerings. Make sure the reports are informative, well-structured, and well-designed to create a positive first impression.

☞ Checklists: Checklists are practical tools that help your audience take action. They are easy to digest and can be used as actionable guides. For example, if you're in the fitness industry, you could provide a workout checklist. If you're in project management, a project planning checklist might be valuable. Checklists simplify complex tasks, making them attractive to your audience.

☞ Templates: Templates are highly valuable because they provide a starting point for your audience. Whether it's templates for spreadsheets, documents, email sequences, or design assets, they save time and effort. Templates also show your audience the practical benefits of your products or services. For instance, if you offer a graphic design course, template design assets can demonstrate your expertise and make it easier for prospects to get started.

☞ Relevance: The key to success is relevance. Ensure that the content you give away aligns with your niche and the pain points of your target audience. By addressing their specific needs and interests, you'll attract prospects who are genuinely interested in what you have to offer.

☞ Building an Email List: Offering these valuable resources in exchange for email sign-ups is a common and effective practice. Building an email list allows you to nurture relationships with prospects over time and guide them toward becoming paying customers.

- Demonstrating Value: Short reports, checklists, and templates demonstrate the value you provide. They show that you're committed to helping your audience and can be a preview of the quality they can expect from your paid products or services.
- Scalability: These types of content are scalable. Once created, they can be easily distributed to a large audience without a significant increase in resources or costs.

Remember to promote your free content through various marketing channels, such as social media, email marketing, your website, and even collaborations with other influencers in your industry. Also, be open to feedback from your audience to continually improve the quality and relevance of the content you offer for free. Over time, as you build trust and a loyal following, you can consider expanding your free offerings and developing a well-rounded content strategy to support your online business growth.

What about using AI to grow your business? How would AI assist you in the creation of short reports, checklists, and templates to attract your ideal clients into your online business?

Using AI to assist in the creation of short reports, checklists, and templates is an excellent way to streamline content creation, enhance efficiency, and provide valuable resources to attract ideal clients to your online business. Here are some ways you can leverage AI for this purpose:

- Natural Language Generation (NLG) tools like OpenAI's GPT-3 can help generate written content, including short reports and articles. You can provide the tool with a topic or outline, and it can generate the content based on your input.
- Use AI-powered tools like Copy.ai or Writesonic to create content, including checklist items, headlines, and descriptions.
- AI-powered design tools like Canva or Crello can assist in creating visually appealing templates for various purposes, from social media graphics to presentation slides.

- ☞ For spreadsheet templates, consider using AI-driven data visualization tools like Tableau or Power BI to create dynamic and informative templates.
- ☞ AI can help personalize content for your ideal clients. You can use AI algorithms to analyze user data and behavior to tailor the content you offer to individual preferences and needs. This can make your content more relevant and engaging.
- ☞ AI tools can be used to proofread and edit your content for grammar, style, and clarity. Tools like Grammarly and ProWritingAid are examples of AI-powered writing assistants that can help ensure your content is error-free and well-written.
- ☞ AI analytics tools can provide data-driven insights into what types of content resonate with your audience. This information can inform your content strategy and help you create content that is more likely to attract and engage your ideal clients.
- ☞ Implement AI-driven chatbots or virtual assistants on your website to engage with visitors, answer common questions, and collect information about your prospects' preferences and needs.

AI tools can help optimize your content for search engines by analyzing keywords, providing suggestions for improving SEO, and ensuring that your content ranks well in search results.

Use AI-driven email marketing platforms to segment your email list, personalize content, and send automated, targeted emails to different groups of prospects based on their interests and behavior.

AI can assist in conducting market research and analyzing your competitors. This information can help you identify gaps in the market and create content that addresses the unique needs of your ideal clients.

AI-driven tools can help you set up and analyze A/B tests to optimize the effectiveness of your content and marketing strategies.

When implementing AI in your content creation and marketing efforts, it's important to maintain a balance between automation and personalization. While AI can streamline processes and enhance efficiency, it's crucial to ensure that your content remains human-centric and resonates with your audience. Additionally, continuously monitor the results of your AI-driven strategies and make adjustments as needed to achieve the best outcomes for your online business.

What about moving the free line as an affiliate marketer? Is the strategy a different one than when you're promoting your own products, courses, and programs?

The concept of "moving the free line" can be applied to affiliate marketing, but the strategy may have some differences compared to promoting your own products, courses, or programs. In affiliate marketing, your primary goal is to promote and sell products or services owned by other businesses. Here's how you can adapt the "moving the free line" strategy to affiliate marketing:

- ☞ Just as with your own offerings, it's essential to choose affiliate products or services that are of high quality and align with your audience's interests and needs. Promoting valuable products enhances your credibility as an affiliate marketer.
- ☞ Produce content that provides value to your audience and showcases your expertise in the niche or industry related to the affiliate products. This content can take the form of blog posts, videos, podcasts, or social media posts.
- ☞ Offer educational content that addresses the pain points and challenges your audience faces. This could include tutorials, guides, reviews, and how-to articles that help your audience understand the benefits of the affiliate products.
- ☞ Create comparison reviews or in-depth product/service reviews that highlight the pros and cons of the affiliate products. Be honest and transparent in your assessments, as this builds trust with your audience.
- ☞ Use the "moving the free line" strategy to collect leads by offering free resources related to the affiliate products. These resources could be free e-books, checklists, or templates that provide valuable information and encourage visitors to subscribe to your email list.

- ☞ Leverage AI and data analytics to personalize your affiliate marketing efforts. Use AI-driven tools to segment your email list and tailor your promotional messages to different subscriber preferences and behaviors.
- ☞ Position yourself as an authority in your niche by consistently offering valuable insights and information. Share success stories, case studies, and real-world examples related to the affiliate products.
- ☞ Always disclose your affiliate relationships and be transparent about the fact that you earn commissions for sales generated through your affiliate links. Honesty fosters trust and helps maintain a positive reputation.
- ☞ Recommend affiliate products in the context of your educational content and recommendations. Tailor your promotions to the specific needs and preferences of your audience, highlighting how the affiliate products can solve their problem.
- ☞ Continuously analyze the performance of your affiliate marketing efforts. Test different content types, promotional strategies, and affiliate products to determine what works best with your audience. Optimize your approach based on the data.

While the fundamental concept of moving the free line remains the same in affiliate marketing – offering valuable free content to attract and engage your audience – the emphasis is on promoting other companies' products or services. Success in affiliate marketing relies on building trust and demonstrating your expertise, similar to promoting your own products, and adapting the strategy to the specific needs of your audience and the affiliate products you're promoting.

SECTION FOUR

HOW DO I BECOME AN EFFECTIVE MARKETER?

"Do what you do so well that they will want to see it again and bring their friends."

~ **Walt Disney**

How does someone new to business learn how to be an effective marketer? This is the question I am most often asked, and it comes when someone has done everything they can think of to build a profitable business and come up short.

Then, they think they have a better way, and when they discover they do not, that is when they are finally ready to listen to me, and to others who have become experts in this area.

Learning to be an effective marketer, especially for someone new to business, involves a combination of education, practical experience, and ongoing refinement of skills. Here's a step-by-step guide to help you get started:

Educate Yourself to Have a Competitive Edge

Read Books and Blogs: Start with foundational marketing books, including classics and contemporary works. Follow reputable marketing blogs to stay updated on industry trends.

- Online Courses: Enroll in online courses from platforms like Coursera, Udemy, or LinkedIn Learning. Look for courses on digital marketing, social media marketing, and copywriting.
- Industry Conferences: Attend marketing conferences and workshops to learn from experts, network with professionals, and gain insights into emerging trends.

One of the primary reasons I began hosting my live marketing conferences, as well as small group Retreats in Santa Barbara was to learn even more and allow others to use my strategies in their businesses. This was a wise proposition for everyone and continues to be valuable on many levels. I highly recommend you look for live events that you may attend at a minimum of twice each year.

Strive to Understand Your Target Audience

- Market Research: Conduct thorough market research to understand your target audience's needs, preferences, and pain points. Use surveys, interviews, and analytics tools to gather data.
- Create Buyer Personas: Develop detailed buyer personas to represent your ideal customers. This helps tailor your marketing messages to specific segments.

Learn Digital Marketing Basics

- SEO and Content Marketing: Understand the basics of search engine optimization (SEO) and content marketing to improve your online visibility.
- Social Media Marketing: Familiarize yourself with major social media platforms and their advertising capabilities. Learn how to create engaging content and run targeted campaigns.
- Email Marketing: Learn the fundamentals of email marketing, including list building, segmentation, and creating effective email campaigns.

Practice Copywriting Skills

- ☞ Study Persuasive Writing: Learn the principles of persuasive writing. Understand how to create compelling headlines, persuasive copy, and effective (CTAs) calls to action.
- ☞ Write Regularly: Practice writing marketing copy regularly. Start a blog or contribute articles to build your portfolio.

Hands-On Experience

- ☞ Internships and Entry-Level Positions: Gain practical experience through internships or entry-level positions in marketing. Real-world experience is invaluable for learning how to apply theoretical knowledge.
- ☞ Freelance Projects: Take on freelance marketing projects to build a portfolio and gain exposure to various industries and challenges.

Networking and Mentorship

- ☞ Join Professional Groups: Connect with other marketers through industry-specific groups on platforms like LinkedIn. Engage in discussions, ask questions, and learn from experienced professionals.
- ☞ Seek a Mentor: Find a mentor in the marketing field who can provide guidance, share insights, and help you navigate your career.

Stay Current on Trends

- ☞ Follow Industry News: Subscribe to marketing publications and blogs to stay informed about the latest trends, tools, and strategies.
- ☞ Continuous Learning: Marketing is an ever-evolving field. Commit to continuous learning through webinars, podcasts, and advanced courses.

Analytics and Data Interpretation

- ☞ Google Analytics: Learn how to use analytics tools, especially Google Analytics, to measure the performance of your marketing efforts.
- ☞ Data-Driven Decision-Making: Develop the ability to interpret data and use insights to make informed marketing decisions.

Build a Portfolio

- ☞ Showcase Your Work: Create a portfolio showcasing your marketing projects, campaigns, and achievements. This will be valuable when applying for jobs or freelance opportunities.

Experiment and Iterate

- ☞ Experiment with different marketing strategies and tactics. Use A/B testing to understand what resonates best with your audience.
- ☞ Learn from Failures: Not every campaign will be a success. Learn from failures and iterate your strategies for improvement.

Soft Skills Development

- ☞ Communication Skills: Hone your communication skills, both written and verbal. Effective communication is crucial in marketing.
- ☞ Creativity: Cultivate your creative thinking. Innovative and original ideas can set your marketing efforts apart.

Certifications

- ☞ Industry Certifications: Consider obtaining relevant certifications, such as Google Ads or HubSpot certifications, to validate your skills.

I began this practice when I was new in the field of real estate, and it served me well in how I was able to grow my business profitably and satisfyingly. The technology I learned as I worked on my ePro certification was probably the most value and made it easier for me to be tech savvy as a classroom teacher and now as a marketer, author, and online entrepreneur.

Remember, becoming an effective marketer is a continuous journey of learning and adaptation. Embrace challenges, stay curious, and be proactive in seeking opportunities to apply your knowledge. The combination of education and hands-on experience will contribute to your growth as a successful marketer.

Several legendary marketers and sales experts have shared their insights and strategies in influential books. Here are some recommended authors and their notable works that can provide valuable perspectives on marketing and sales:

Seth Godin...

Recommended Book: "Purple Cow: Transform Your Business by Being Remarkable"

Godin's work focuses on the concept of making your business remarkable and standing out in a crowded marketplace.

Al Ries and Jack Trout...

Recommended Book: "Positioning: The Battle for Your Mind"

This classic book delves into the importance of creating a strong position in the minds of consumers and how to differentiate your brand.

David Ogilvy...

Recommended Book: "Ogilvy on Advertising"

Why Read: Often referred to as the "Father of Advertising," Ogilvy shares timeless principles and insights from his experience in the advertising industry.

Gary Vaynerchuk...

Recommended Book: "Jab, Jab, Jab, Right Hook: How to Tell Your Story in a Noisy Social World"

Why Read: Vaynerchuk provides insights into effective social media marketing and the art of storytelling in the digital age.

Simon Sinek...

Recommended Book: "Start with Why: How Great Leaders Inspire Everyone to Take Action"

While not a traditional marketing book, Sinek's work emphasizes the importance of starting with the "why" in marketing and business communication.

Zig Ziglar...

Recommended Book: "Secrets of Closing the Sale"

Ziglar is a legendary sales expert, and this book provides practical advice and techniques for closing sales effectively.

Brian Tracy...

Recommended Book: "The Psychology of Selling"

Tracy's book explores the psychological aspects of selling and provides actionable strategies for success in sales.

Dale Carnegie...

Recommended Book: "How to Win Friends and Influence People"

While not specifically about sales, Carnegie's classic work on human relations is foundational for anyone in sales or business.

Grant Cardone...

Recommended Book: "Sell or Be Sold: How to Get Your Way in Business and in Life"

Cardone shares his high-energy approach to sales and provides insights into the mindset of successful salespeople.

Jeffrey Gitomer...

Recommended Book: "The Little Red Book of Selling: 12.5 Principles of Sales Greatness"

Gitomer's book is packed with practical tips and principles for achieving sales greatness. In this book, Gitomer shares practical advice, principles, and strategies to help sales professionals enhance their effectiveness and achieve success in their sales endeavors.

He is widely recognized as an expert in the field of sales. He is a seasoned sales professional, speaker, and author known for his dynamic and engaging approach to sales training and education. Gitomer has written several best-selling books on sales, business, and customer service, and he is a popular speaker at sales conferences and events.

Key aspects of Gitomer's approach to sales include building relationships, understanding customer needs, effective communication, and a focus on providing value to clients. His work often emphasizes the importance of mindset, attitude, and ongoing self-improvement in the field of sales.

In addition to "The Little Red Book of Selling," Gitomer has authored several other books, including "The Sales Bible," "Customer Satisfaction is Worthless, Customer Loyalty is Priceless," and "Little Gold Book of YES! Attitude."

Overall, Jeffrey Gitomer's contributions to the field of sales, his engaging speaking style, and his practical insights make him a respected authority in the sales and business community.

Peter Drucker...

Recommended Book: "The Practice of Management"

Drucker's insights on management and business strategy have had a profound impact. This book covers essential principles for effective business management.

Michael Porter...

Recommended Book: "Competitive Strategy: Techniques for Analyzing Industries and Competitors"

Porter is renowned for his work on competitive strategy. This book provides frameworks for analyzing industries and gaining a competitive edge.

Tom Peters...

Recommended Book: "In Search of Excellence: Lessons from America's Best-Run Companies"

Peters explores the practices of excellent companies, offering valuable lessons in business excellence.

Remember to adapt the insights from these books to your specific industry and context. Reading a variety of perspectives can help you form a well-rounded understanding of marketing and sales principles. While we're on this topic, be sure to take a look at all of the books I've written, or co-authored with others.

Chapter 12

My World... And Welcome to It

"In this ever-changing society, the most powerful and enduring brands are built from the heart. They are real and sustainable. Their foundations are stronger because they are built with the strength of the human spirit, not an ad campaign. The lasting companies are those that are authentic."

~ Howard Schultz

As you might have realized by now, I have created a world that provides me with a lifestyle by design. That term was first coined by Tim Ferriss and I embraced the concept immediately to start creating the life I had wanted for many years, believed I honestly deserved, and now knew how to turn it into my reality.

What about you? Have I convinced you to embrace marketing in a way that makes sense for you? Are you gently persuaded to release any negative energy you may have been carrying regarding asking people to buy from you? Will you now read sales copy as someone who understands the goals of the copywriter and the needs and desires of the prospect?

If you answered "Yes!" to even one of these questions, that means my words and those of my co-authors have not fallen on deaf ears. It also means you are on your way to building a business of great proportions and with stellar potential, whether it's online or a brick-and-mortar company.

The Study of Marketing

Over the years, I've encountered and made friends with people who are experts in marketing, sales, and persuasion. These are people I previously would not have had much of an interest in getting to know on a deeper level. I had many misconceptions going into these friendships, and am extremely thankful I got past those limiting beliefs and grateful for how these relationships have made a difference, not only for me but also for the people I mentor in one of my two programs.

The ongoing study of marketing is a worthwhile one for you, even if you haven't yet started your business.

World and Community Building

The concepts of world building and community building can be powerful marketing strategies for entrepreneurs and small business owners, particularly in today's interconnected digital landscape. Let's break down each concept and how they can be utilized.

> World building involves creating a rich and immersive environment around your brand or product. It's about crafting a narrative, setting, and aesthetic that draws customers in and makes them feel connected to your brand on a deeper level.
>
> As an entrepreneur, you can utilize world building by developing a compelling brand story that resonates with your target audience. This could include creating fictional characters (this is known as creating an avatar), building a unique visual identity, and establishing a consistent tone and voice across all marketing channels.
>
> > Example: A bookstore might create a brand identity centered around the idea of a cozy, rustic cabin in the woods, with imagery, packaging, and messaging that evoke feelings of warmth, comfort, and nostalgia.
>
> Community building involves fostering a sense of belonging and connection among your prospects, customers, or followers. It's all about creating spaces and opportunities for people to engage with each other and with your brand, forming relationships, and building loyalty.
>
> Entrepreneurs and small business owners can effectively build community through various channels, such as social media platforms, online forums, email newsletters, and in-person events. Encouraging interaction, providing valuable content and

resources, and actively listening to feedback are key components of community building.

Example: A yoga business might host regular workout challenges on social media, where customers can share their progress, connect with each other, and receive support and encouragement from the brand.

The benefits of world building and community building include:

- ☞ Differentiation: Building a distinctive world and community around your brand helps you stand out from competitors and create a unique identity that resonates with your target audience.
- ☞ Brand Loyalty: By fostering a sense of belonging and connection, you can cultivate a loyal customer base who are more likely to return to your business and advocate for your brand.
- ☞ Word-of-mouth Marketing: Your fully engaged community members are more likely to share their positive experiences with others, leading to organic word-of-mouth marketing and increased brand awareness.

Building a community provides a valuable feedback loop, allowing you to gather insights directly from your customers and make informed decisions about product development, marketing strategies, and customer service.

A strong brand world and community can provide a solid foundation for long-term growth and sustainability, as loyal customers become ambassadors for your brand and help attract new customers over time.

You can now see that world and community building are powerful marketing strategies that allow entrepreneurs and small business owners to create deeper connections with their customers, differentiate themselves in the market, and build a sustainable and loyal customer base.

By investing time and resources into crafting compelling narratives, fostering engagement, and nurturing relationships, businesses can position themselves for success in the digital age. This is a Big Deal for everyone.

Partnering With Your Prospects, Customers, and Clients

As an introvert, I honestly believed I could sit in front of my computer and build a six-figure business all by myself. Instead, I learned that forming relationships was an absolute necessity if I wanted to succeed. And in the process, I've made lifelong friends and grown to seven figures along the way.

These days, I teach relationship marketing as part of every course and program I create. I encourage my mentees to make friends early on so they'll have people in their corner, and vice versa as their businesses grow.

It's much like what I experienced as a classroom teacher: Everyone feels alone on the first day of school. But all it takes is for someone to smile at you and say "Do you want to be my friend?" for that to turn around.

This all leads me to sharing with you why I continue to partner with my prospects, clients, and mentees.

All ships rise when you create a team of two or more people. Ideas flow, creativity spikes, and the next thing you know you've come up with a winning idea. This was the case when I connected with a man who came into my mentoring program with an idea for sharing concepts in a way that went beyond joint venturing.

We spent weeks practicing what he had thought out, and I added my own take on the topic. Then, I reached out to my long-time friend and colleague, Dr. Jeannette Cates to see what she thought about it. I met Jeannette the first year I came online – 2006 – and when I joined the Mastermind and mentoring group she was a part of as a marketing and course creation advisor, we became fast friends.

Jeanette had some excellent ideas on how we could position this product and training and we went on to earn six figures with this over the next 12 months.

You'll also want to empower others around you. This is referred to as thinking eternally or celestially and requires you to be spiritually minded with what you say and do each day.

Over the years, I've begun to think of everyone in my life, whether they live close by or far away from me on another continent, or even if I know them only virtually, as already having reached and achieved what they are striving for in their life and business.

If it weren't for the people who treated me in this way long ago, I might not have ever had the courage and belief in myself that I needed to succeed not only in my business but also in my personal life.

I went on to create more courses and programs with Jeannette, including our popular "Dot Com Jumpstart" and "JVs Made Simple."

Connect with people in person and virtually to see who you most resonate with when it comes to your business. Then, suggest a simple product or course you could create and sell together. This would be a joint venture (JV) and not a legal partnership. This way it's a simple process to continue doing business together in the way that is working for each of you, or to simply go your separate ways and remain as friends and colleagues. Having one person in the partnership work as an affiliate of the other is also a strategy that works effectively.

Chapter 13

Readers Are Leaders and Marketers Are Influencers

"Everyone thinks of changing the world, but no one thinks of changing himself."

~ Leo Tolstoy

Your Message is Powerful

Your message makes a difference to everyone you encounter. Now you may be thinking, "Message? What message do I have that could make a difference for anyone else?" I had the same thoughts when I began my journey as an online entrepreneur and marketer back in 2006. But I was determined to succeed, so I asked questions of others and created a simple plan as a way to begin.

As a former classroom teacher, I thought back to what I did to motivate and inspire my students to excel in their academic studies. I used to order books from Scholastic and other book clubs, as well as check out books from the local library. Using my "teacher" card allowed me to borrow more books and keep them longer because they were to be used in the classroom.

I hung a poster in the back of the classroom that proclaimed "Readers Are Leaders!" and had it laminated so it could be used year after year. I placed this poster above the sink so that anyone who took a drink of water or washed their hands would easily see it. I thought of this as a subliminal message, like the ones at the movie theaters that encourage you to buy candy, popcorn, and drinks during the previews. Now that's a marketing strategy to discuss sometime!

This concept of readers being leaders was so deeply ingrained in my mind that once I came online, one of the first things I did was plan out my reading schedule.

At this point in my life, I had become accustomed to reading for pleasure several times a week. When we had SSR (Silent Sustained Reading) after lunch each day in the classroom, I would typically read right along with my students.

Sometimes there was a distraction, like when another teacher or an administrator would come to the door and needed to speak with me. But other than that, I always had a book or two with me.

I was enjoying John Grisham and Elmore Leonard novels. I had wanted to become an attorney when I was younger and even went to law school for a year and a half before deciding it wasn't right for me, so I lived vicariously through the stories Grisham told.

Many of Elmore Leonard's stories were set in South Florida, where I had lived during my teenage years, and I loved the experience of vicariously exploring and revisiting these locations through the eyes of his characters.

But after teaching and working in real estate simultaneously for close to twenty years, I was now starting my own business online.

I quickly realized that what I truly needed was more of a business education. I promised myself that I would only read books related to the topics I now needed to learn about and that I wouldn't read any fiction for a minimum of one full year.

This proved to be a wise decision on my part and one that helped me to advance in my field of marketing, content creation, and entrepreneurship more rapidly. Yes, I now read fiction regularly and even write my own stories that are based more on fiction than on truth, but the ever-evolving story of how I transitioned to writing scripts and screenplays is a story for another day.

The next goal I set was to keep everything simple. I saw too much complication in everything I was doing and was determined to make it all as doable as possible. This led me to learn more about minimalism and simplicity and that's how I found out about Wabi-Sabi. This strategy continues to make a difference in my life's journey.

Embracing Wabi-Sabi: A Marketer's Guide to Simplicity and Authenticity in the Digital World

In the fast-paced realm of Internet marketing, where algorithms evolve, trends emerge, and information overload is a constant companion, finding peace and balance seems like an elusive goal. As marketers, we're often entangled in the pursuit of perfection, striving for an unattainable ideal that leaves us drained and dissatisfied.

Enter Wabi-Sabi, an ancient Japanese tradition that beckons marketers to reevaluate their approach, embrace imperfection, and find beauty in simplicity. In a world dominated by digital noise, understanding and applying the principles of Wabi-Sabi can be a game-changer.

Wabi-Sabi, at its core, values imperfection, transience, and authenticity. These principles are not merely aesthetic preferences but a profound way of thinking that can be seamlessly integrated into the digital marketing landscape. Imagine simplicity, humility, and an appreciation for imperfection – that's the "Wabi" aspect. Couple it with an acknowledgment of the passage of time and the impermanence of all things – that's "Sabi."

This philosophy has long been a cornerstone of Japanese culture, influencing everything from tea ceremonies to architecture. However, its relevance is not limited to the East; it has found resonance in Western design and art. Think of the rise of minimalist design and the trend of upcycling – both inspired by Wabi-Sabi, emphasizing simplicity, functionality, and the beauty of imperfection.

For internet marketers, the benefits of incorporating Wabi-Sabi principles are multifaceted. Accepting imperfection becomes paramount in a landscape where algorithms can be unpredictable, and campaigns may not always go as planned. Gratitude for the present moment is crucial amidst the constant flux of digital trends and consumer behaviors. Mindfulness is indispensable when navigating the intricacies of online engagement.

Consider the environmental consciousness aspect of Wabi-Sabi – valuing the use of natural materials and appreciating the beauty of the natural world. In the digital age, where sustainability is a growing concern, adopting this philosophy can make marketers more aware of their environmental impact and guide them toward more sustainable choices.

Creativity and self-expression, core elements of Wabi-Sabi, align seamlessly with the dynamic nature of internet marketing. Embracing a unique style and creativity rather than conforming to trends can set a brand apart in the crowded digital space.

So, how does this philosophy translate into the daily life of internet marketers? Imagine infusing your digital presence with the essence of Wabi-Sabi.

In your digital space (Your Website)

Embrace simplicity in website design, focusing on clean layouts and easy navigation.

Opt for authenticity in content creation, sharing behind-the-scenes glimpses, and embracing the imperfections that make your brand human.

In your digital campaigns (Your Work)

Strive for authenticity in your marketing messages. Share real stories, celebrate successes, and learn from failures.

Embrace imperfection in the constantly evolving digital landscape. Adapt and iterate, rather than striving for a perfect but static strategy. This strategy alone will change your life and your perceptions about what is possible and how you can create your own lifestyle by design.

In your online engagement (Your Relationships)

Value authenticity in building relationships with your audience. Focus on meaningful connections rather than chasing superficial metrics.

Embrace the impermanence of digital trends. Cherish the current moment and adapt your strategies as the online landscape evolves.

The principles of Wabi-Sabi, when applied to internet marketing, can significantly reduce anxiety and stress. Letting go of the pursuit of perfection, focusing on the present moment, finding beauty in simplicity, and embracing impermanence – all contribute to a more resilient and adaptable approach to digital marketing.

As you can see, Wabi-Sabi is not just a philosophy; it's a transformative mindset for internet marketers. It encourages us to embrace imperfection, find beauty in the digital world's natural ephemerality, and appreciate the fleeting nature of trends and algorithms.

By infusing our digital strategies with Wabi-Sabi principles, we can create more authentic connections with our audience, reduce stress, and foster a sense of resilience in the ever-evolving landscape of internet marketing. Cheers to simplicity, authenticity, and the beauty of imperfection in the digital age!

How Are You Embracing the Beauty of Imperfection and Simplicity in Your Life and Business? Tadao Ando's Story

In 1995, a massive earthquake struck Kobe, the seventh most populous city in Japan. It registered 7.2 magnitude on the Richter Scale. More than six thousand people were killed, thirty thousand injured, and another forty-five thousand people were left homeless.

Yet, there was one area where not a single building was damaged or even had a crack...

Days later, architect Tadao Ando made his way through the streets, navigating away from first responders helping residents through the debris, and climbing through the rubble to find the neighborhood where more than thirty buildings he had designed were located. As he stopped in his tracks and stared at each one in turn, he realized that out of the entire area affected by the earthquake, his buildings were the only ones that were still standing tall and strong.

Born in 1941 in Osaka, Japan, he first studied as a boxer and a fighter. While on a high school trip to Tokyo, the young Ando stumbled across Frank Lloyd Wright's Imperial Hotel, and he was instantly struck by the power of architecture. Less than two years after graduating from high school, he ended his boxing career to pursue architecture.

Tadao Ando is a self-taught architect. Raised by his great-grandmother after his parents decided they would not be able to raise both Tadao and his identical twin brother, Takao Kitayama, Tado flourished under their care. There would never be enough money for him to have a college education, but they encouraged and nurtured his interest in architecture and the arts. He attended night school, took correspondence courses, and visited buildings designed by renowned architects located all over Japan.

He knew why his structures had survived the devastating earthquake. After studying and becoming one of the few self-taught architects in the world, he had always emphasized the connection between nature and architecture.

Characteristics of his work include large expanses of unadorned architectural concrete walls combined with wooden or stone floors and large windows, and he is best known for his minimalist concrete structures. He often uses concrete planes to play with light and space while harmonizing the building with its natural surroundings. He is truly honoring the beauty of imperfection and simplicity in his work.

In his own words, Ando goes deeper:

We do not need to differentiate one from the other. Dwelling in a house is not only a functional issue but also a spiritual one. The house is the locus of the heart (Kokoro), and the heart is the locus of God. Dwelling in a house is a search for the heart (Kokoro) as the locus of God, just as one goes to church to search for God.

An important role of the church is to enhance this sense of the spiritual. In a spiritual place, people find peace in their heart (Kokoro), as in their homeland.

Ando's style with the buildings he designs create a haiku effect, emphasizing nothingness and empty, negative space to represent the beauty of simplicity. He favors designing complex spatial circulation while maintaining the appearance of simplicity and absolute minimalism.

Ando believes that if you give people nothingness, they can ponder what can be achieved from that nothingness. Active natural elements, including the sun, rain, and wind are also a part of his style.

In my work as a mentor and trusted advisor to people who want to emulate the lifestyle and business I've created for myself, moving past perfection is always the elephant in the room. Learning that perfection only exists in nature helps all of us to move forward with our goals and dreams.

I highly recommend Adam Grant's approach, and his explanation of "wabi-sabi" is a beautiful model to embrace. This worldview is centered on the acceptance of simplicity and imperfection. I'm at conniegreenhouse at Yahoo dot com and would be interested in knowing your thoughts on this.

"Hidden Potential: The Science of Achieving Greater Things" by Adam Grant is changing how I think about almost everything!

Embrace the impermanence of digital trends. Cherish the current moment and adapt your strategies as the online landscape evolves. Do not have fear around anything new, such as artificial intelligence. Remember that people have feared computers for decades, as they did with electricity and cars.

The principles of Wabi-Sabi, when applied to internet marketing, can significantly reduce anxiety and stress. Letting go of the pursuit of perfection, focusing on the present moment, finding beauty in simplicity, and embracing impermanence – all contribute to a more resilient and adaptable approach to digital marketing.

Tadao Ando's architectural philosophy is deeply influenced by the principles of Wabi-Sabi, a Japanese aesthetic that embraces imperfection, simplicity, and the transient nature of things. While Ando may not explicitly reference Wabi-Sabi in his work, the underlying ethos of this philosophy is evident in many aspects of his life and architecture.

Here are several ways in which Tadao Ando incorporates Wabi-Sabi principles into his life and work. Keep an open mind and a softened heart as you discover some ideas that may be new to you...

Simplicity and Minimalism

Wabi-Sabi emphasizes simplicity, and Ando's architectural designs reflect this by featuring clean lines, uncluttered spaces, and a minimalist aesthetic. His buildings often strip away unnecessary ornamentation, embracing a simplicity that allows the essential qualities of materials and spaces to shine.

Imperfection and Authenticity

Wabi-Sabi values imperfection and authenticity. Ando's use of raw, exposed concrete in his designs is a prime example. Instead of concealing the imperfections of the material, he celebrates them, showcasing the natural textures and irregularities of concrete. This authenticity adds a human touch to his structures.

Harmony with Nature

Wabi-Sabi encourages a connection with nature, and Ando's architecture seeks harmony with the natural environment. Whether it's integrating a building with a garden, incorporating natural light, or designing spaces that interact with the landscape, Ando's work aligns with the Wabi-Sabi appreciation for the beauty found in the natural world.

Acceptance of Transience

Wabi-Sabi acknowledges the impermanence of all things, and Ando's designs often reflect this acceptance of transience. The patina that develops on materials over time, the play of light and shadow that changes throughout the day – these elements contribute to an understanding that buildings, like all things, evolve and age gracefully.

Attention to Craftsmanship

Wabi-Sabi places value on craftsmanship and the human touch in creation. Ando, in his pursuit of perfection within imperfection, collaborates with skilled craftsmen to achieve precision in the execution of his designs. This attention to detail and the human hand in the construction process aligns with the Wabi-Sabi emphasis on the beauty of the handmade.

Curation of Experience

Wabi-Sabi extends beyond physical aesthetics to the experience of a space. Ando carefully curates the sensory experience within his buildings, considering not only the visual aspects but also the sounds, textures, and atmosphere. This holistic approach reflects the Wabi-Sabi appreciation for the totality of an experience.

While Tadao Ando may not explicitly label his approach as Wabi-sabi, the resonance of its principles in his architecture is unmistakable. His work embodies timeless simplicity, an acceptance of imperfection, and a deep respect for the interplay between the built environment and the natural world – all fundamental tenets of the Wabi-sabi philosophy.

Embracing the Beauty of Imperfection and Simplicity as a Marketer and Entrepreneur

Tadao Ando's beliefs around Wabi-Sabi hold valuable lessons for marketers and entrepreneurs, offering insights that can guide their approach in the dynamic and competitive business landscape. Here's how Ando's Wabi-Sabi philosophy is relevant to marketers and entrepreneurs and why it is my sincere hope that you take the time to put at least some of these ideas and concepts into practice in your own life and business to discover what is possible...

Embracing Imperfection

Wabi-Sabi encourages the acceptance of imperfection as a source of beauty. Marketers and entrepreneurs can apply this principle by acknowledging that perfection is often unattainable. Embracing imperfections in products, campaigns, or processes can lead to authenticity and relatability, fostering stronger connections with the audience.

Simplicity in Messaging

Ando's minimalist designs reflect simplicity, a key aspect of Wabi-Sabi. Marketers can adopt this by simplifying their messaging. Clear, straightforward communication resonates better with audiences bombarded by information. A simple message is more likely to be understood and remembered. If only I had learned and embraced these principles early on in my business, everything would have unfolded much differently for me.

Authenticity Builds Trust

Wabi-Sabi emphasizes authenticity, and marketers can build trust by embracing their brand's authentic identity. Consumers appreciate honesty and transparency. Highlighting the imperfections and unique qualities of a brand can create a more genuine connection with the audience.

Harmony with Audience Needs

Ando's focus on harmony with nature can be translated to marketers seeking harmony with their audience. Understanding and aligning with the needs, preferences, and values of the target market creates a harmonious relationship. It involves adapting strategies to resonate with the audience rather than imposing a rigid approach.

Connection with the Environment

Wabi-Sabi encourages a connection with the natural world. Marketers can adopt a similar mindset by considering the environmental impact of their strategies. Sustainability and eco-friendly practices not only align with Wabi-Sabi principles but also appeal to the growing consciousness of environmentally conscious consumers.

Timeless Appeal

Ando's designs have a timeless quality, transcending trends. Marketers can strive for the same timeless appeal by focusing on enduring values rather than chasing short-lived trends. Building a brand that stands the test of time involves consistency, reliability, and an appreciation for the lasting impact of authentic connections.

Attention to Detail

Wabi-Sabi places value on craftsmanship and attention to detail. Marketers and entrepreneurs can apply this by paying meticulous attention to every aspect of their brand – from product design to customer service. A focus on quality and the finer details contributes to a positive and memorable customer experience.

Cultivate Meaningful Experiences

Wabi-Sabi extends beyond aesthetics to the experience of a space. Similarly, marketers can focus on curating meaningful experiences for their customers. This involves considering not only the product or service but also the overall customer journey, ensuring that every touchpoint contributes to a positive and memorable experience.

Incorporating the principles of Wabi-Sabi into marketing and entrepreneurial endeavors can lead to more authentic, human-centric, and sustainable practices. By embracing imperfection and simplicity, practicing gratitude and forgiveness, and maintaining a harmonious connection with the audience and environment, marketers and entrepreneurs can create lasting and meaningful relationships with their customers.

The Influence We Wield as Marketers

Although as marketers we sometimes feel like others in the world of business do not truly understand us, the truth is that humans are more alike than they are different, at least in my experience. Having influence may feel wonderful at times, but it must never be taken for granted or abused.

We've all known, or at least heard of someone who became drunk with power as a result of something that occurred in their life experience. That's never pretty, and serves as a reminder to us to think before we speak, act, or inflict our beliefs upon others.

The goal is to add to the positive parts of what we experience on earth, and to make our presence one that will illuminate the world in some way, I believe.

SECTION FIVE

WHAT'S NEXT?

"There is nothing more tragic than to find an individual bogged down in the length of life, devoid of breadth."

~ Dr. Martin Luther King Jr

Your New Life as a Marketer

We must ensure that the length of our lives does not outstrip the breadth. As a marketer, you hold the power to lead your life in a very different way than those who leave the marketing to others.

My Story as to How I Became a Marketer

I've shared much about myself throughout this book, but now I'd like to go deeper with my story. It sometimes sounds like a fairy tale or other made-up story when I share it aloud with someone, and over time it feels more and more like I'm telling someone else's story instead of my own. But it is indeed the life I have been able to create for myself and a lifestyle by design.

First of all, I want to say that I honestly believe this is the best business and lifestyle on the planet. When I made the conscious decision to find a way to resign from my classroom teaching job at the end of the following school year and to simultaneously give away my long-time real estate clients in search of a new life experience, the stakes were high.

My mother was in her eighties and had taken a fall that left her unsteady on her feet and needing my help more regularly. She received a social security check that barely paid her rent and I was the only one who could supplement her income every month for everything else she needed.

If I carried out my plan, that would leave me vulnerable in terms of money coming into my bank account. Also, I wanted to move to a new city about 30 miles north of where I was living, and that would make the stakes even higher. It meant that I would have to start over in real estate and that another school district wouldn't be likely to hire me, even as a substitute due to my age and previous health issues as a cancer survivor.

Not only were the stakes high, but I had no idea how I would actually earn income on the internet. Others were doing it, but perhaps they knew lots more than I did. In fact, I was SURE they did.

But the other side of the coin told the rest of the story... I was exhausted from working more than 60 hours a week, always just a few months from depleting my savings, and had no one to help me if this new online business didn't work out. I was also a multiple cancer survivor and worried about a recurrence.

I made a plan. This included starting to learn about online entrepreneurship by listening to CDs while driving, starting a blog and posting twice a week, finding a few affiliate products to promote, and reaching out to others online and introducing myself. As an introvert, that was by far the most difficult part of my plan.

When I made my first affiliate sale, I danced around the room like I'd won the lottery. Someone I didn't know had clicked on my link and purchased! That was enough encouragement for me to continue with my plan...

This included refinancing my house to squeeze every bit of equity out of it, giving notice to the school district that my last day would be on June 30th, and making the move to the new city.

As the school year moved closer to the end, I was both excited and terrified for the future. I had faith it would all work out and kept putting one foot in front of the other. That summer I had to start paying for my health insurance for the first time since I had become an adult.

My plan continued. Each day I wrote a 250-to-300-word post for my blog. About 24 hours later, I'd add the post to one of the article directories. There was a link for people to join my list, as well as a link to an affiliate product. Then, I would read and listen to anything I could find to help me learn more about how to earn income online.

It wasn't easy, but I was determined. By the end of the summer, I knew that I needed help. That's when I cashed out my retirement account from the school district and hired a mentor to work with me.

I did not tell anyone what I had done. But I have no regrets and have now been mentored non-stop for close to 18 years. I had too much to lose by NOT changing my situation, so it made sense for me to make the jump and give it my best shot.

Over these years, my life has changed completely. And I promised myself long ago that as soon as I knew what I was doing, I'd send the elevator down to help others move up to closer to where they want and need to be to change their lives as well. This continues to be a joyous and fulfilling process and I am honored to work with those who trust me to guide them in this way.

I hope it's obvious to you from what I'm sharing with you here that I absolutely LOVE the life and business I've created online. I was slowly suffocating while I was in the workforce and longed for a life that could make sense for me.

A chance encounter with someone I met at a real estate conference led me to an evening seminar about starting a business on the Internet. That was in 2005 and a year later I was ready to resign from the school district and turn my real estate clients over to others who could better serve them.

Not only had I never been mentored at that time in my life, I also had never known anyone who had mentioned working with a mentor. But a few months online attempting to figure it out all on my own led me to the conclusion that a mentor was exactly what I needed if I was going to replace my previous income and build a business I would be proud and excited to be a part of each and every day going forward. I've been living the mentored life since that time and cannot imagine ever going it alone again.

How about you? Are you happy about how your business is moving forward? Do you look forward to connecting with people from around the world who are interested in how you will serve them? Do you feel cared for and supported by people who understand what it's like to be an online entrepreneur and marketer?

I began my "Incubator Mastermind" mentoring program when I reached a consistent six figures a year in my business. I was 18 months in and knew there were people who would benefit from mentoring with me. I kept the group small, worked privately with each person, and brought everyone - no more than 20 people in any given year - together at least a couple of times a month. You'd recognize the names of some of the people who got their start with me.

Two years later I opened up a monthly mentoring program. We met via webinar two or three times a month and they had priority email access to me. Over time, some people stopped attending live, and others no longer watched the replays. I knew it was time to make some changes. Some people joined the "Incubator Mastermind" as openings became available. I gave the others four months' notice and closed the monthly mentoring program.

In August of 2023 I opened a new version of my "Monthly Mentor Program" and people began joining the group. You may want to take a look at how I have this program set up and what it's all about at https://MonthlyMentorProgram.com

I'm so very proud of each person. They're working hard, setting up websites/blogs, creating content, getting to know one another, and asking questions. Half of them have at least a simple product or course available for sale!

And my Incubator Mastermind has now evolved as well. It is now called the Strategic Alliance Mentoring Partnership for Perfected Ascension, or SAMPPA for short.

Chapter 14

Do for a Year What Others Won't

"Do for a year what others won't; Live, forever the way others can't."

~ **Connie Ragen Green**

"Have you started your year?" I ask this question regularly of the people I mentor. Many of them struggle with consistency, creativity, and productivity, which keeps them from achieving the goals and dreams they had when they originally came to me.

What about you? Do you believe you can do anything you set out to do? Or, do you think, at least down deep that others are more able to be successful than you will ever be?

This is the "Enough" syndrome and we have all struggled with this at some point in our lives.

For me, it began when I was in elementary school and one day realized that my mother and I were poor. But it was about more than not having enough money for the basic necessities of life; it was also about feeling as though I wasn't worthy of having nice things or achieving extraordinary goals.

I expanded on this dialogue as I got older. I was continually discovering new areas where I came up short.

Taking It All in Stride

Even though I had attained some level of success, at least in terms of what many people – Americans at least – use to judge one's worth, these insecurities continued to be rooted deep in my brain and I just couldn't shake them.

In 2005, I had a reawakening of sorts and decided that I wanted to create a new life for myself. I began attending personal development seminars and reading books that made me think about myself and my life experience in a very different way.

In one session, we were asked to write down what we had accomplished in our life that we were proud of for any reason. That evening, I excitedly made a list of everything I could think of that was a part of my life.

I'd graduated from UCLA with honors, gone on to attend Law School in New York City, and then decided not to become an attorney. Then I had worked as a claims adjuster for a national insurance agency, passed my real estate exam – on the second try – and worked in real estate until deciding to return to college to earn a teaching credential and became a classroom teacher.

Just writing all of this here leaves me breathless, as I had accomplished all of this before I had celebrated my 30th birthday.

But that's where my forward motion had stalled out. What had caused this? As I thought about it, I concluded that I had become fearful of what the future held for me. At that point, I had begun second-guessing everything I was doing or wanted to do. I stopped trusting myself to make decisions that would be best for myself. And, I began to live each day as though it might be my last. This fear was sucking the breath out of me and causing me to feel like I had nowhere to turn.

How did I overcome these invisible obstacles and discover the joie de vivre of life once again? The answer was right in front of me all the time. I needed a new reason to live my life to the fullest and to serve others with what I would learn so they would benefit as well. This showed up for me when I learned that people just like myself were starting businesses on the internet, and that I could be a part of this world by jumping in, learning as much as I could about the basics of online marketing, and then taking action every day to put everything into place.

Every job I had ever taken allowed me to serve others in some way. I served those who had suffered personal or property losses while I was a claims adjuster. As a real estate broker and residential appraiser, I served people who needed my help with the services I could provide for them. And as a classroom teacher, I served not only my students, but also their families in a myriad of ways.

Now I was ready to embark on a journey that would take me all over the world and stretch my mind to new depths, all in pursuit of the secrets of marketing, sales, and persuasion. And after almost twenty years, I now understand that this is a field I will never get tired of or grow out of for any reason, as this world continues to morph in ways no one could have ever predicted.

Don't Overthink It – It's Just Sunglasses!

Every few months I find myself making the four-and-a-half-hour trek from my home in southern California over to Las Vegas. Sometimes I go there to speak at or to attend someone's marketing event, for years it was twice a year to host my own Weekend Marketer Workshop (I moved this event to Manhattan Beach, California several years ago), and once in a while, it's just to see a show and enjoy some time away from my business with friends, family members, or even by myself.

No matter what takes me there, I always enjoy stretching my legs at the outlet stores about a hundred miles outside of Vegas.

On my most recent trip I stopped at the Tanger Fashion Outlets to make a phone call, check my email messages, and take a short break before continuing for the last ninety minutes or so of my drive. I wasn't looking for anything in particular so I went into a shoe store to browse, used the restroom, and headed back to the other side of the parking lot to get going on my way once again. I walked by the sunglass outlet store, checked my watch to make sure I was still on schedule and ducked inside for a quick look.

First, I'll give a little history about me and sunglasses. Years ago, I learned that it was important to protect our eyes from the sun's harmful UV rays, so I vowed to always wear quality sunglasses when I was out in the sun. Over the years I would purchase two pairs on sale, and then carefully use them interchangeably until they were both completely worn out.

I'm proud to say that I have only lost one pair during my entire life, and that is most probably because I use one of those leather eyeglass leashes at all times to keep track of them. That one time, they must have slipped out and dropped without my knowledge.

About a month before this most recent trip my last pair broke in a way that could not be repaired (one of the arms snapped in the middle), causing me great pain as I lamented the loss of sunglasses I truly loved. This led to my going online to search for a quality pair to replace them, but I was shocked at the prices and kept putting it off. I had been wearing an old pair I had stuffed away in my sock drawer but really wanted a brand-new pair of polarized, UV glasses that would serve me well for the next few years.

So, when I entered the outlet store on that sunny spring day and breathed in the smell of designer plastic, I was in heaven. Four young sales girls stood ready to help me and one of them moved in closer to greet me. I told her I was looking for a pair of Ray-Bans, and she directed me to a corner with about a dozen pairs on display. As I tried on several pairs, I carefully looked at the price tag before sliding them atop my nose. I wasn't about to fall in love with something way out of my price range.

At some point, I was aware of a woman about my age observing me interact with the sales girl. I was just about to thank the girl and head out of the store when the woman approached us. I still had the last pair of glasses in my hand when she spoke.

"Those seem a little sporty, don't you think?"

I was taken aback. I could be sporty. It was possible. Who was this person, commenting on my taste without even knowing me?

"Yes, I like sporty", I found myself mumbling. I was looking down and enjoying my last seconds with the sunglasses that would not be mine.

"Your coloring is similar to mine. That color frame will wash you out and make you appear yellowish".

"Oh?" The ones I was holding were the most gorgeous shade of light green.

"You'll want something darker, and that model of Ray Bans doesn't offer UV protection, either."

I slipped them back onto the display case and slowly said, "I could be sporty, and I like that style."

The woman, who still had not identified herself to me, moved in closer and stared me down.

"Then you'll want these."

She thrust a pair at me, and I could clearly see the word "Oakley" on their rim. Her outstretched arm revealed a delicate gold bracelet with the initial "J" at the top.

"They are perfect for your coloring, are polarized and have UV protection, and because they are a discontinued style, they are only sixty-two ninety-nine today. They normally retail for two hundred forty dollars."

She stepped back, and I was suddenly aware that my mouth was open. Who was this woman? She had observed that I was brand driven, price conscious, and obviously in need of a new pair of glasses, all within a few minutes.

"I'm Jill, the manager of the store. Let me show you something else."

"Thank you", I stammered, feeling like I had been reduced to a glob of jelly in her presence. She was good at this.

Jill held up a picture of a parrot in a small frame. Without sunglasses, the picture was gray and flat and dim. She motioned for me to put on the Oakley sunglasses again and I obeyed. Instantly the parrot was brightly colored and seemed to have three-dimensional texture as well.

I reached out to touch it, sure that it was some kind of magic. We were pretty close to Las Vegas.

"How does it do that?" I asked.

"It's the polarization, protecting your eyes from the sun's harmful rays and letting the safe, natural light in."

I was dumbfounded. This was polarization? I thought I knew what that was, but Jill was educating me about this in a way that felt comfortable and not like I was a dummy.

"Many people confuse polarization with UVA or UVB protection. It's a natural mistake." She held the parrot picture up at a different angle and my eyes followed.

Jill had disarmed me completely, rendering me childlike in my responses. I was putty in her hands. I did the only thing I could, reaching inside my purse for a credit card.

"I'll take them."

She smiled knowingly and gestured for me to follow her to the cash register. I again noticed the four young salesgirls, who were studying this encounter as though the details of it were going to be on an exam after I left the store.

"You'll also want this cleaning kit."

She held open a small brown box, pulled out a cloth, sprayed it with something, and expertly wiped the glasses clean, all within about ten seconds.

"Yes."

It was all that I could say, and I hoped it didn't cost too much. Again, she read my mind.

"It's only four ninety-five, and you can take it to any of our stores nationwide for free refills."

Of course, you could! Jill knew her products like she knew the back side of her hand, and more importantly, she knew people.

I could not resist finding out more about who she was and why she happened to be in the middle of the desert selling sunglasses.

For the next twenty minutes or so Jill and I talked about what had just happened. She was not a salesperson by trade, but after being downsized by one company and laid off by another she finally took this job to make ends meet. It turned out she was a natural, and soon this store became the top-selling one in the territory. I'm not sure how many states that might cover, but it sounded huge the way she described it.

She broke down her philosophy for me in a few short sentences...

"I tell the girls to observe the customer for a few minutes before moving in. They quickly find out their wants and needs and also their objections. Then they make a couple of recommendations and wait for the customer to respond. I tell them to not overthink it; it's just sunglasses!"

Yes, indeed. I learned a little about polarization and a lot about salesmanship on this day that I won't soon forget.

Recently, I went for my annual appointment with the ophthalmologist, with the intention of getting a pair of prescription sunglasses. As a marketer, I am keenly aware of how people at any business will lead me through the process of making a final purchase. Usually, I'm not impressed by the steps they take to move me from where I was originally to where I'll be when I leave the establishment.

This team of people, from the person who greeted me when I first arrived, to the doctor, and everyone in between did an outstanding job, and I ended up ordering three new pairs of glasses as a result.

Why is this so important? We must observe our own and other's behavior, both face-to-face and online, in order to better understand how to interact with the prospects who will be considering the products, courses, and programs we create.

The next time you're in the market to make a purchase, think of yourself in slow motion, as if you're walking through a vat of Jello or pudding. What are you thinking at each step in the process, what comes next, and what happens when you finally make a purchase, or decide to walk away?

We will always be our own best Case Study, and I encourage you to pay attention to how you react, behave, and finally take action (or not) with everything that comes into your life experience. It's fun, and will most definitely increase your bottom line in your business.

Knowing Exactly What to Market to Your Prospects, Customers, and Clients... Mind Reading

This morning I was thinking about what it was like when I first came online and was finally ready to create my first product. I had learned so much, yet I wasn't sure what to offer the hundred or so people who had joined my list.

I ended up creating a simple, three-part training on how I was writing short blog posts on topics I knew something about, posting them to the article directories 24 hours later, and including an affiliate link to a relevant product or course at the end of each article/post. I believed others would want to know how to do this, so I launched the product/course and crossed my fingers.

A few people did come aboard, but not as many as I had hoped to attract. It turned out that the people on my list were more interested in learning other things, but even when I asked in my emails, very few people told me exactly what they wanted to spend their time and money on to achieve their goals.

Over the next couple of years, I figured out what they wanted to learn and buy from me with a little more clarity, but I continued to wish I had a foolproof method of reading the minds of people on my list to better serve them.

It's worthwhile to take the time and make the effort to learn how to create products and services your customers can't wait to buy. It makes everything much easier and your income will continue to stay on track, even during downturns in the economy or your marketplace.

Have you ever worked really hard on the "best idea in the world" only to have nobody buy it? Or even worse, just one or two people buy and you end up losing money on the time you end up spending for such a small group.

This is exactly what happened to Geoff, a client of mine who became a close friend and writing partner. I had invited him to accompany me to Atlanta for a marketing conference. I was hosting a breakout event the day before and asked him to present his ideas and research on copywriting to those who were planning on joining me that day. We were a group of about forty newer marketers and entrepreneurs, and they loved what he shared with them for about an hour. At the end of his talk, he said he was going to create a product on what he had come up with and that it would be available for sale within the next two weeks.

I was there every minute and several people told him they could not wait to buy this new training. He told everyone in the room that they would be able to buy it for 50% off because they had been so excited about it.

You can probably guess what happened. He created the training on writing sales copy using his strategies and methods and set it up on a sales page with all of the details. He priced it at forty-nine dollars, which was more than fair, and then emailed everyone who had been in Atlanta with a link to the page and a coupon code to come aboard for half off – twenty-four dollars and fifty cents.

We spoke two days later and he gave me the news. Crickets. Not even one person emailed him back to ask him more questions about the product or to tell him why they weren't going to purchase it after saying they would just over two weeks earlier.

Then on the third day one person purchased. I told him to send one more email to everyone, telling them they had three more days to come in for half off before he would be emailing his entire list with the offer at the full price.

No one else purchased it, and when he sent it out to everyone, he only made two sales.

Understanding what to market and offer for sale to your prospects, customers, and clients is crucial for business success. While direct feedback from customers is valuable, there are several strategies you can employ to identify market needs and tailor your offerings effectively:

Conduct thorough market research to understand industry trends, customer behaviors, and emerging opportunities. Analyze competitor offerings and identify gaps or areas where you can differentiate your products or services.

Use surveys and feedback forms to gather insights directly from your existing customers. Ask about their preferences, pain points, and what improvements they would like to see in your offerings.

Monitor social media platforms for discussions, comments, and mentions related to your industry and products. Analyze the sentiment of these conversations to understand what customers appreciate and what concerns they have.

Conduct one-on-one interviews with your customers to gain in-depth insights into their needs and experiences. Focus on open-ended questions to encourage detailed responses.

Utilize data analytics tools to analyze customer behavior on your website or app. Look for patterns, popular products, and areas where customers may be dropping off in the purchasing process.

Stay informed about industry trends, technological advancements, and changes in consumer behavior. Anticipate future needs and position your offerings accordingly.

Attend industry conferences, trade shows, and networking events to stay connected with professionals and potential customers. Gain insights into emerging trends and challenges.

Develop buyer personas based on demographic, psychographic, and behavioral characteristics. Tailor your marketing strategies to address the specific needs of each persona.

Test new products or features with a select group of customers before a full launch. Gather feedback and make adjustments based on the results.

Be flexible and adaptable to changing market conditions. Regularly review and update your offerings based on customer feedback and market dynamics.

By combining these approaches, you can develop a comprehensive understanding of your target market and align your products or services with the needs and preferences of your customers. Regularly reassessing and adjusting your strategies will help you stay responsive to changing market demands.

Imagine what it would be like to have a crystal clear picture of your "tribe" and be able to offer them exactly what they want (so you can give them what they need to succeed?) You can do this without spending a lot of time or money, and in the process, you'll be learning more about your target audience than you ever thought would be possible.

You'll be honing in on the exact pain points and beliefs your audience has regarding your topic, and this knowledge is invaluable over time. Remember, when you begin your marketing journey, you are most likely creating a business that would serve you. That's right, we create what we most need, and so the process begins. You grow along with your prospects, until you finally progress to the next stage in the process.

Creating an Avatar of Your Ideal Client?

I have discovered that creating an avatar and bringing it to life is an extremely valuable use of my time about once each year.

Creating an avatar, also known as a customer persona or buyer persona, involves developing a detailed and fictional representation of your ideal client. This persona helps you better understand your target audience, tailor your marketing strategies, and align your products or services with their needs. Here's a step-by-step guide to creating an avatar of your ideal client:

Collect data on your existing customers, including demographics, psychographics, and behavioral patterns. Use customer surveys, interviews, and analytics to obtain insights into their preferences, challenges, and motivations.

Identify different segments within your target audience based on characteristics such as age, gender, location, income, interests, and buying behavior. Prioritize segments based on their importance to your business.

Develop individual personas for each segment by combining common traits and behaviors. Give each persona a name, job title, and a face that will stay top of mind (you can use stock photos to represent them visually).

Define the persona's age, gender, location, income level, education, and other relevant demographic details.

Explore the persona's interests, hobbies, lifestyle, values, and attitudes. Understand their goals, challenges, and aspirations.

Analyze the persona's buying behavior, including their decision-making process, preferences, and factors that influence their choices.

If applicable, include details about the persona's job title, industry, company size, and professional goals.

Determine how your persona prefers to communicate, whether through social media, email, phone, or in-person meetings.

Identify the common challenges and pain points your persona faces. Understand how your products or services can address and solve these issues.

Define the persona's short-term and long-term goals. Understand what motivates them and how your offerings can contribute to their success.

Develop a narrative or story that encapsulates the persona's background, challenges, goals, and how your products or services fit into their journey.

Many online tools and templates are available to guide you through the persona creation process. These templates often include sections for demographics, psychographics, goals, challenges, and more.

Periodically revisit and update your personas as your business evolves or as you gather more information about your target audience.

By creating detailed avatars of your ideal clients, you can humanize your target audience, making it easier to tailor your marketing messages and strategies to effectively reach and engage them. Regularly revisit and update these personas to ensure they remain reflective of your evolving customer base.

I hope that you are now ready and willing to do for a year what others will not, as the notion of living for the remainder of our lives the way others cannot keeps me on my toes and excited to be alive during this period of history.

Chapter 15

The Great Divide: Email Marketing and Artificial Intelligence

> *"If you don't have at least ten thousand people on your list, no one will take you seriously, you can't be a player in the online space, and you won't make much money."*
>
> **~ Marketer from 2006 who disappeared soon after making this statement; possibly taken by alien beings to a galaxy far away**

When I started my online business back in 2006, I was already accustomed to communicating via email. I had begun with Prodigy in 1986 and I can remember that they allowed you to send up to thirty messages each month. This was because no one at the time could imagine why you'd ever need to send more than that. I'd send a message to one of my friends, and then call them up and tell them to turn on their computer and log in to Prodigy to see what I had written.

Yes, it was primitive, but it was a start and the beginning of something big... Very BIG.

The quote at the beginning of this chapter is from someone who has since disappeared from the online space. When I first heard what he had said and truly believed, my response came quickly and without hesitation...

"I'm sure glad I didn't get that memo. I got to six figures with 651 names on my list, and my business and income continue to grow."

Yes, I made a name for myself with what I said, and I wasn't even trying to do anything more than respond to his mistaken belief. Finding your voice, speaking your mind, and not fearing controversy or retribution is crucial to success.

I have a few more than 651 people on my list these days, but every one of them holds a place of gratitude and respect in my heart and mind. Instead of ever thinking of someone as a number, we must imagine them as a fully fleshed-out human being, with desires and needs similar to our own and the potential to be someone we consider as being very special in our life experience.

Building a list, and then communicating regularly with those people is crucial to creating an online business that will provide you with an opportunity to live a "lifestyle by design" that many of us have come to love and appreciate.

Seth Godin, thought leader and marketer extraordinaire recently shared his thoughts on email, artificial intelligence, and asking the questions that will make a difference...

For what purposes will it be useful?

"In 1840, at the dawn of the information age, the king of Sardinia asked Charles Babbage what nearly instant messaging like the telegraph could possibly be good for.

Twenty years later, it was obvious.

When I first saw Prodigy in 1986, I saw that the consumer internet would have many possibilities, but I didn't have the guts to ask what I was missing. 'In 40 years, for what purposes will it be useful' would have been a productive way to think about the change that was happening.

AI is as big a change as the internet, perhaps more so. And in just a few years, people will wonder why we weren't wondering better."

~ Seth Godin

Seth Godin has a reputation for asking the hard questions, the ones others dismiss before they exit the mind in favor of more mundane ideas.

Email Marketing as a Profitable Strategy

I had an account with Compuserve in 1989 when they first launched. Our accounts were labeled by a series of numbers instead of with your name. Compuserve identifiers are in the form 12345,1234; however, you cannot include a comma in an Internet email address. Compuserve had designed it so you could replace the comma with a period for this purpose. Furthermore, you must be sure to include your domain as well, so a properly formatted Compuserve Internet email address would be "12345.1234@compuserve.com". Perhaps they wanted it to resemble a Stardate, but I don't know that for sure.

Prodigy had already launched, as I described at the beginning of this chapter and I was excited to join and discover what they were sharing in this new age of digital awareness and technology.

I so wanted to bring this into my classroom as a new teacher, but the school district had little understanding of the process or the purpose of making it available for the students.

We went back and forth for several months in 1986, and the final conversation was an odd one, where I finally agreed with the person on the other end of the phone line that a telephone in an elementary school classroom was not a good idea. I already had three computers in my classroom, with the first one being an Apple IIe provided by Steve Jobs and Steve Wozniak of Apple to every 5th grade classroom in California.

The following year I wrote a technology Grant that was chosen and funded by the school district.

It would be several years later that the Internet was finally brought into the public school system I was a part of in Los Angeles, but even when I resigned in June of 2006 they were still behind the times with technology.

AOL was my next stop for an email account, but they made it clear they were going to censor every word that we sent or received and I had no interest in being a part of that world.

In 1998, CompuServe was acquired by America Online and most of us moved on.

Yahoo started providing email accounts at no cost in the fall of 1997. It was called Yahoo! Mail and I created an account right away. Overnight, it seemed like everyone was communicating via email and we were checking our virtual inboxes as regularly as possible so we wouldn't miss anything.

Google launched Gmail in 2004 and offered everyone a storage capacity of one gigabyte per user at no cost. Not being someone who liked to compare and choose, I had both a Yahoo! and a Gmail account and set about learning how to best utilize them for personal use, as well as for my teaching job and my real estate business.

At some point, I became aware of people I knew having email accounts connected to the domain for their business, as a type of branding. It would be several years before I followed suit and these days I have several email addresses on my servers.

As I mentioned above, embracing and practicing the skill of sending emails to others was a crucial part of fast-tracking my learning curve with email as well as technology overall.

When I speak with other authors, I like to ask a question I already know the answer to: Do you have a list? They will quickly share that they have a website, but when I again ask them specifically if they have a way for visitors to their website, as well as those they know and people they encounter in their day-to-day life to give them their name and email address to join a permission-based list, the answer is almost always that they do not.

Herein Lies the Ensuing Conundrum, Leading to the Great Divide

Although everyone whom I encounter online will agree that communication through an email list is effective as a marketing strategy, the overwhelming majority of these marketers remain firm in their beliefs that emailing every day is too often. We all choose our path as entrepreneurs, but it has always made sense to me to listen to and learn from those who are succeeding in an area where I need some guidance.

This is an article I published on the topic of email marketing for beginnings, where you can learn more about why I believe email marketing is a crucial part of marketing...

Email Marketing for Beginners

Email marketing can be a very intimidating aspect of becoming an online entrepreneur. It is a process where you are asking permission to take someone's name and email address, something very personal to many people, and contact them on a regular basis. I'll share my experiences with email marketing for beginners with you here.

You may have many different questions and concerns about integrating email marketing as a part of your overall strategy for success. If you are new to this process, you will want to learn a variety of things such as the basic technical steps, the strategic options you have, and the etiquette that needs to be considered when communicating with your list.

Below, you will find the answers to ten of the most common questions about email marketing. This will provide you with a solid foundation to get started so that you can stop wasting time and build a list that is eager to hear your expertise and insight.

The longer you put this task off, which is a common obstacle for many, the more you are delaying profits and branding that could elevate you to the next level of success as an online marketer.

What Is Email Marketing?

For those who are brand new to the concept and don't know what email marketing is, it's a strategy of communicating with your target audience directly in their inbox rather than waiting for them to approach you on your blog or on social media platforms.

Many marketers use email marketing to showcase their expertise as a niche leader, to promote products and services (either as a vendor or affiliate), and to serve the needs of their audience.

You can drive traffic to your blog, to sales pages, or to your social media accounts. Ideally, you'll be doing a combination of informing, educating, and entertaining your audience through your email autoresponders.

This is one of the best ways to level up your business because it's a cost-effective strategy that builds momentum over time. It lets you build a strong rapport with your subscribers and most systems give you a plethora of analytical data so that you can improve your conversions over time.

How Do I Build a List of Subscribers?

Before you start sending out emails, you have to have someone to send them to, right? In order to build a list of subscribers, you have to go through a process that begins with narrowing down your target audience.

Not everyone in the world is going to want to be on your list. So, think of who your demographic is. Are they men – or women? What age group are they? What interests do they have?

Once you know more about them, you can create a lead magnet that will be of use to them. This can either eliminate a pain point or obstacle – or it can be used to elevate their life to the next level, helping them achieve a goal they've set for themselves.

Your lead magnet offer can be a report or video course. It might be a series of emails that are drip-fed to subscribers over the course of a week or more. Try not to rely on the simple, stale statement of, "Sign up for updates," because you need a stronger incentive to convince people to hand over their contact details.

You need to make it easy for people to sign up. A first name and email address will suffice. Don't start asking for their mailing address and phone number (or even their last name) because you will lose many subscribers if you do. Think about it: The last thing you want to do when you're connecting with someone new, especially online is to share every personal detail with them. I ask for their first name and best email address and leave it at that.

Putting your opt in form on its own landing page where you can drive traffic to it strategically. But also include it below each blog post, so that if someone enjoys your content, they can immediately sign up to your list.

You also want to have the opt in form in the sidebar of your blog so that people can see it on every page of your site when they are navigating around. There are some platforms that allow you to build a list from your profile, such as a Facebook page, so be sure to integrate that there.

Sometimes, there will be a niche giveaway event that you can take part in. Numerous marketers all find something they want to give as a free gift and everyone drives traffic to the site.

Your listing can send people to your opt in page where the leads can sign up as subscribers and download their gift. You also want to make sure that if you sell a product on a platform like Warrior Plus, that you have your autoresponder system connected so that buyers are sent a confirmation email to get on your list.

What Email Autoresponder System Should I Use?

Your email autoresponder is the system you'll be using to gather the contact information of your subscribers and then queue up emails to be sent out to them. You want to choose the best one that's right for you.

They all have individual pricing plans, but the great news is – most have a free option for newbies to begin building momentum with their list before they pay anything. AWeber and GetResponse are two of the most popular autoresponders that are perfect for newbies. I've used AWeber since my second year online (2008) and highly recommend you get started with their free plan to begin with, as a way to ease into the habit of emailing regularly. Email marketing for beginners does not have to be painful or confusing. Once you get used to this part of online marketing and entrepreneurship, you'll be on your way to a life changing business.

With AWeber and also with GetResponse, you can use their system free for up to 500 subscribers. By that time, you'll be earning income online and it will make sense to pay the $19 per month for their full, professional service plan.

They each have their own type of system that can include templates you can customize, landing page builders, segmentation and data analysis provided, and more. If you know you want to integrate your autoresponder somewhere specific, make sure that the platform you're considering will work with that.

Some people primarily base their first choice for an email autoresponder system on how much it costs them. But you have to think long-term. It's not a fun or easy process to migrate an entire list over to a new platform, so you want to choose something you'll be happy with as you grow your list.

What Kinds of Emails Should I Send to Subscribers?

There are different types of emails you can send, along with different styles (like longer or shorter emails). You will find the best way to communicate with your target audience, and it needs to be genuine for you – not a spammy, false persona.

Authenticity is important. But you can also control the types of emails you send out to people. This is something that stumps many individuals. They build a list and then have no idea what to say to them.

The very email you're going to create is a welcome email. This not only tells them that you're happy to have them as a new subscriber, but it provides them with the access link to the free gift they were promised when they signed up.

After that email is written, you need some marketers go with a simple newsletter. This can include a variety of items where you discuss trends and news in your niche, offer insight or tips about how to do something, share updates or progress on products, and so on.

You can also send emails where you only do one of those things, rather than having multiple items in the email. Promotional emails are where some marketers get intimidated.

You want to make sales and commissions, but you don't know how to sell in an email. Promote products, services, and courses that you feel are truly worthy to your subscribers – and protect their interests at all costs.

Your email should cover briefly the benefits they'll enjoy, the reason you feel it's a good fit for them, and what your specific thoughts are if you reviewed it. Make sure you abide by all rules for emailing out about a product as an affiliate.

You also might want to occasionally survey your subscribers. This is especially helpful if you are creating info products and want to tailor it to their needs. Use a tool like SurveyMonkey for this purpose.

If you have any type of event, like an upcoming online webinar or in-person meet up, you can make an announcement in your email letting people know so they can attend that.

There's no perfect email marketing strategy that will suit everyone. But you will learn, over time, what your subscribers do and don't respond to – and you'll be able to make the privilege of having their contact information work in your favor, as long as you treat them well. Remember to bookmark and return often to this detailed information on email marketing for beginners.

Let's move on now to the next part of what I refer to as The Great Divide... Artificial Intelligence. Unlike email which has been around for almost four decades and is now in the mainstream of society, the use and understanding of artificial intelligence is still in its infancy.

Artificial Intelligence and the World of Online Marketing

AI may have crept into our lives on little cat feet, but it has landed as a prehistoric beast towering over us in unknown ways. I'll paraphrase the quote I shared earlier from Seth Godin on this topic:

> *AI is as big a change as the internet, perhaps more so. And in just a few years, people will wonder why we weren't wondering better.*

Artificial intelligence has been around for decades. Let's take a look at the history, move into the present time, and surmise what the future could look like for entrepreneurs and marketers interested in utilizing AI in their businesses.

The history of artificial intelligence (AI) is indeed fascinating and multifaceted, with numerous developments shaping its trajectory from theoretical concepts to practical applications. Building upon the foundation laid out in your excerpt, here's a continuation of the narrative along with key milestones:

Early Development and Turing's Legacy

Alan Turing's pioneering work laid the groundwork for AI by posing the question of whether machines could exhibit intelligent behavior. His concept of the Turing Test, proposed in his 1950 paper, remains influential in AI research today.

Turing's ideas spurred further exploration into the mathematical and computational aspects of intelligence, leading to the development of early AI algorithms and theories. It was new and exciting and some were ready to learn more.

Emergence of AI Programs

Following Turing's work, researchers began to explore practical implementations of AI. One notable early program, apart from the Logic Theorist, was the General Problem Solver (GPS) developed by Newell and Simon in 1957. GPS aimed to solve a wide range of problems using heuristic search techniques.

These early AI programs laid the foundation for the development of more sophisticated AI systems in the decades to come.

AI Winter and Resurgence

Despite initial optimism, the field of AI faced setbacks in the late 1960s and 1970s, leading to what became known as the "AI winter." Progress stagnated due to challenges such as limited computing power, lack of data, and unrealistic expectations.

However, interest in AI resurged in the 1980s with the advent of expert systems, which employed knowledge-based approaches to problem-solving. Expert systems found applications in various domains, including medicine, finance, and engineering.

Machine Learning and Neural Networks

The late 20th century saw significant advancements in machine learning, a subfield of AI focused on developing algorithms that improve automatically through experience.

Neural networks, inspired by the structure of the human brain, gained prominence as powerful tools for pattern recognition and classification tasks. Breakthroughs such as the backpropagation algorithm enabled more efficient training of neural networks.

Modern AI Technologies

In recent years, AI has witnessed rapid progress fueled by advances in deep learning, big data, and computational resources. Deep learning, a subset of machine learning, has revolutionized tasks such as image recognition, natural language processing, and speech synthesis.

Applications of AI permeate various industries, including healthcare, finance, transportation, and entertainment. Autonomous vehicles, virtual assistants, and recommendation systems are just a few examples of AI-powered technologies shaping the modern world.

Ethical and Societal Implications

Alongside technological advancements, discussions surrounding the ethical implications of AI have gained prominence. Concerns about job displacement, algorithmic bias, privacy infringement, and autonomous weapons have sparked debates and calls for responsible AI development and deployment.

Efforts to ensure transparency, accountability, and fairness in AI systems are ongoing, with organizations and policymakers working to establish guidelines and regulations for ethical AI usage.

Overall, the journey of AI from its conceptual origins to its current state reflects a blend of scientific inquiry, technological innovation, and societal impact. As AI continues to evolve, it presents both opportunities and challenges that will shape the future of humanity.

Unlocking the Power of Artificial Intelligence: A Journey from Fantasy to Reality

In the ever-evolving landscape of technology, few advancements have captured the imagination quite like artificial intelligence (AI). From its humble beginnings as a concept in science fiction to its present-day ubiquity, AI has undergone a remarkable transformation, revolutionizing industries and reshaping the way we live and work.

The seeds of AI were sown in the early 20th century through the imaginative works of writers and filmmakers who envisioned a world populated by intelligent machines. Who could forget the iconic Tin Man from "The Wizard of Oz" or the humanoid robot Maria from "Metropolis"? These early depictions laid the groundwork for the exploration of AI as a scientific and philosophical concept.

However, it wasn't until the brilliant mind of Alan Turing entered the scene that AI began to take shape as a tangible field of study. Turing's groundbreaking 1950 paper, "Computing Machinery and Intelligence," challenged the notion of human exceptionalism by proposing that machines could, in theory, exhibit intelligent behavior. His ideas sparked a wave of curiosity and exploration, paving the way for further research into the mathematical and computational principles underlying AI.

The journey from theory to practice was not without its challenges. In the early days, computers could not store commands, limiting their ability to exhibit true intelligence. Moreover, the exorbitant cost of computing made experimentation and innovation prohibitively expensive. It wasn't until the landmark Dartmouth Summer Research Project on Artificial Intelligence in 1956 that the tide began to turn.

At the Dartmouth conference, visionaries like John McCarthy and Marvin Minsky brought together top minds from various disciplines to discuss the future of AI. While the conference fell short of its lofty expectations, it galvanized a generation of researchers and laid the foundation for decades of progress.

Since then, AI has experienced both peaks and valleys, with periods of rapid advancement followed by periods of stagnation. However, recent years have seen an explosion of interest and investment in AI, driven by breakthroughs in machine learning, neural networks, and big data.

Today, AI is no longer confined to the realm of science fiction; it is a tangible force driving innovation across industries. From personalized recommendation systems to autonomous vehicles, AI-powered technologies are transforming the way businesses operate and interact with their customers.

As entrepreneurs and marketers, it's essential to recognize the potential of AI as a tool for growth and differentiation. By harnessing the power of AI-driven insights and automation, businesses can unlock new opportunities for efficiency, personalization, and customer engagement.

However, with great power comes great responsibility. As we embrace AI, we must also be mindful of its ethical and societal implications. From concerns about algorithmic bias to the ethical use of data, it's incumbent upon us to ensure that AI is deployed in a manner that respects privacy, fairness, and human dignity.

We now know that the journey of AI from fantasy to reality is a testament to human ingenuity and perseverance. As we stand on the cusp of a new era of innovation, let us seize the opportunities that AI presents while remaining vigilant in our commitment to ethical and responsible use. Together, we can harness the power of AI to build a brighter, more prosperous future for all.

The Future: What Will AI Look Like for Marketers, Writers, and Entrepreneurs?

The future of AI holds immense promise for marketers and entrepreneurs, offering a wealth of opportunities to drive growth, enhance customer experiences, and streamline operations. Here are some key aspects of how AI is expected to shape the landscape for marketers and entrepreneurs:

Data-Driven Insights

AI-powered analytics will enable marketers to gain deeper insights into customer behavior, preferences, and trends. By analyzing vast amounts of data in real time, AI algorithms can identify patterns, predict future outcomes, and uncover valuable insights that inform marketing strategies and decision-making.

Personalized Marketing

AI-driven personalization will become increasingly sophisticated, allowing marketers to deliver highly tailored and relevant content to individual consumers. By leveraging data on past interactions, purchase history, and demographics, AI algorithms can optimize marketing messages, offers, and recommendations for maximum impact.

Chatbots and virtual assistants powered by AI will play a central role in customer service and support. These intelligent systems can handle routine inquiries, provide instant responses, and even assist with product recommendations or purchases, thereby enhancing customer satisfaction and driving conversions.

AI algorithms can predict customer behavior and identify potential leads or opportunities with a high likelihood of conversion. By analyzing historical data and market trends, AI can help marketers and sales teams prioritize their efforts and allocate resources more effectively, ultimately driving higher ROI.

AI technologies such as natural language processing (NLP) and generative models can automate content creation and curation processes. From writing blog posts and social media captions to curating personalized product recommendations, AI can help marketers scale their content efforts while maintaining quality and relevance.

AI-powered tools and technologies will enable marketers to deliver seamless and personalized customer experiences across channels and touchpoints. From website personalization and email marketing to omnichannel campaigns and loyalty programs, AI can help businesses engage customers more effectively and build stronger relationships over time.

AI algorithms can optimize advertising campaigns by analyzing performance data in real time and making adjustments accordingly. Whether it's targeting the right audience segments, optimizing ad creatives, or allocating budget effectively across channels, AI can help marketers achieve better results and maximize ROI.

As AI becomes more prevalent in marketing and entrepreneurship, ethical considerations will become increasingly important. Marketers and entrepreneurs must be mindful of issues such as data privacy, algorithmic bias, and transparency in AI-driven decision-making to ensure that their practices are ethical and responsible.

The future of AI for marketers and entrepreneurs is one of innovation, efficiency, and opportunity. By embracing AI technologies and leveraging their capabilities strategically, businesses can gain a competitive edge, drive growth, and deliver exceptional value to their customers in the digital age.

However, in the realm of AI-driven copywriting and marketing, several concepts and approaches have been explored by various professionals and researchers. Some common areas of focus and concepts include:

Natural Language Generation (NLG)

This involves using algorithms to generate human-like text based on input data. NLG can be utilized in creating product descriptions, blog posts, advertisements, and more.

AI enables marketers to personalize content at scale by analyzing user data and behavior. Tailoring messages to individual preferences and demographics can lead to more effective marketing campaigns.

- ☞ AI tools can analyze vast amounts of data to identify trends and optimize content for maximum engagement. This includes optimizing headlines, images, and even the timing of posts for different audiences.
- ☞ AI-powered chatbots can engage with customers in real-time, providing information, assistance, and even making recommendations based on user queries and behavior.
- ☞ By analyzing past data and trends, AI can predict future consumer behavior, allowing marketers to anticipate needs and adjust strategies accordingly.
- ☞ AI can optimize advertising campaigns by targeting the right audience, selecting the best ad formats, and adjusting bids in real time to maximize ROI.

Many entrepreneurs, copywriters, and marketers have explored or experimented with AI tools and technologies in their work. The field of AI-driven copywriting has seen significant advancements and adoption in recent years, and it is still growing and changing as the world decides how to benefit from its use.

My long-time friends and colleagues Joe Vitale and Jim Edwards are two well-known copywriters who have explored the use of AI in their work, particularly in the realm of sales copy and marketing. Here's a bit about each of them and their involvement with AI:

Joe Vitale is a prolific author, speaker, and copywriter who has written numerous books on marketing, including "Hypnotic Writing" and "The Attractor Factor." He's also known for his work in personal development and spirituality. Vitale has been an advocate for using AI tools in copywriting to streamline the process and enhance effectiveness. He has experimented with various AI-powered platforms and has shared insights and strategies for integrating AI into copywriting workflows.

Joe wrote and published a book in the spring of 2023 using artificial intelligence that you may enjoy reading. It's titled "The Pursuit of Tranquility: The Secret Dialogues of Seneca and Epicurus" and this is what he said about it...

"Seneca and Epicurus never met. The dialogues in this book were imagined by GPT-4, a popular AI program, using my questions as the prompts. Marcus Aurelius, and Ralph Waldo Emerson, never wrote their intros to this book, either. It was all imagined by GPT.

I wanted to see what might be created by stimulating the AI program and sitting back and receiving the results. I was so impressed with the dialogues, and gained so much entertainment and education from them, that I figured this might be worth sharing with the world. Much like a good novel can bring expanded awareness as well as joy, this series of fictional dialogues may also enrich us."

Jim Edwards: Jim Edwards is another prominent figure in the world of copywriting and marketing. He's the co-author of the book "Copywriting Secrets" and the creator of various software tools aimed at helping marketers and entrepreneurs improve their copywriting skills. Edwards has also delved into the realm of AI-driven copywriting, exploring how tools like AI content generators can be used to generate sales copy, email sequences, and other marketing materials more efficiently.

Both Vitale and Edwards have spoken about the potential benefits of AI in copywriting, including its ability to save time, generate ideas, and optimize messaging for better engagement and conversions, contributing to the growing conversation around AI's role in the field of copywriting and marketing.

Chapter 16

Inspired Actions Around Marketing

"The three most important days in the life of a marketer include the day they are born, the day they discover the magic of marketing, and the day they realize they have always had a natural affinity with marketing, sales, and persuasion that has the potential to change not only their life but the lives of those they interact with each day."

~ **Connie Ragen Green**

I'm going to share an article with you here. It describes my early efforts with marketing and is titled *Welcome to Onramp View Estates...*

It was the summer of 1983 and I had passed the real estate exam on my second attempt. The first time I had failed by five questions and told myself I probably wasn't smart enough to be in real estate. A close friend told me that was just "stupid thinking" and encouraged me to try again.

I believed the second test, a different version administered six weeks to the day later in a stuffy downtown Los Angeles high rise, was easier than the first. I never said that out loud and just counted my lucky stars that I was now ready to start my career as an agent with Gribin von Dyl's Sherman Oaks office.

Ira Gribin and Lou von Dyl owned the company and Ira's son Steven was in charge of sales training. Each morning for four weeks I climbed the stairs to the training room on the third floor. I did not realize at the time how fortunate I was to have connected with this group of smart and dedicated people.

Three years later they sold their eight offices throughout southern California in a landmark multi-million-dollar deal but by that time I had moved on to another office and was ready to take the exam to become a broker in my own right.

This was all before technology became commonplace in offices and before the Internet was a part of everyone's daily life. It was also before I truly understood the value of marketing and its effect on almost everything related to business.

But this story is about what happened *after* I graduated from the Gribin von Dyl sales training. It had been a rigorous four weeks and I was ready to get started. As an introvert, my strategy was to stay out of the spotlight and not make any sudden moves to call attention to myself.

My first goal was to arrive early and get my desk set up. We shared desks and I had been assigned a locking top drawer on the left-hand side. I quickly realized how awkward this would be and began counting the days until I could have the coveted top middle drawer or at least the top drawer on the right side. I slid my papers and a small hairbrush into the drawer, closed it tightly, carefully pulled out my key, and stood up to look around.

The office was arranged into cubicles and sections. Mine was in the middle of the office, meaning that I could not see out the plate glass window facing the street or even out the back door that was always left wide open without standing up and moving several feet to the right or left. I did see some people talking in a small group and went over to introduce myself.

They were pleasant enough and each one shook my hand while saying their name. I noticed that they spoke slowly and carefully, as though they believed my hearing wasn't good or that English was not my native language.

They asked what I had done before coming into real estate and I thought before answering and then gave them an abbreviated version of my adult life. I shared that after college I had worked as a merchant teller at a commercial bank and also as a claims adjuster at Liberty Mutual Insurance, one of the largest in the country. But I wanted to be in real estate so I took the exam and here I was.

They were not impressed, or so it seemed to me and excused themselves. One woman remained and she took the time to speak with me. Her name was Molly and she had been in real estate for forty years.

Now I was a twenty-something and could not imagine myself standing in this office forty years from today. But where would I be at that time in my life? I did not have any idea. I just knew that I wanted to be involved in the world of real estate to help others to have a home and to begin investing for myself. Molly then asked me a question I had not previously thought about answering for myself, or even thinking about for that matter.

"Have you saved up enough money to pay your bills for at least the next six months?"

Her eyes softened as she waited for my reply. Her sweet smile landed on me just right and I knew I could trust her. I now had a friend in real estate.

"No. But Ira and Lou and even Ira's son, Steven said we could have a listing and a sale during our first month if we followed the steps they shared with us and followed through regularly."

I knew I sounded like a commercial for Gribin von Dyl's real estate training program. They had sold me on the wonderful world of real estate and the wondrous life of a sales agent and I was excited, if also a little nervous to begin.

"Yes, that's true." Molly lowered her eyes and then looked at me dead on. She didn't say anything more and I had learned in my sales training that the next person to speak in this situation loses.

We both sat down on the dark brown vinyl sofa in the waiting area. The traffic on Ventura Boulevard was whizzing by on this hot August day while we were safely cocooning inside the air-conditioned office. This also might mean fewer people would be coming in during the six hours of "floor time" I had been assigned for each week. But now that thought felt small compared to what Molly was attempting to tell me. She finally broke the silence.

"Even if you make a sale or take a listing today, the deal is not likely to close escrow for at least two months, even during the best of times. Interest rates are going up right now so transactions are taking a little longer."

She went silent again, allowing me to take this all in and prepare for my next question.

"So, what do I do?"

I laboriously got up from the sofa and let out an audible sigh. Now I felt dejected and wished I hadn't gotten into this conversation in the first place. My mind drifted to taking a part-time job at a department store or even working a few shifts each week at a coffee shop. I needed to bring in some money and if that was two months away, or even longer that just wouldn't do.

Molly was on her feet again, mirroring my body language in what I would later learn as a classic sales move that works to build rapport with your clients.

> ***"There is always a solution to every situation."***

She hadn't used the word problem so I was once again hopeful for my real estate career to sustain me.

Silence again. Molly was teaching me as she tortured and teased without words and I succumbed to her lesson.

Over the next half hour, she taught me more about sales, marketing, real estate, and myself than I ever thought could be possible in so short a time. Then we took a short bathroom and coffee break and agreed to reconvene in fifteen minutes.

I returned to my desk and unlocked my personal drawer. From it, I withdrew a small book which I presented to Molly in both outstretched arms when we met up again.

She held it up to the light from the plate glass window as if it held a secret phrase that could not be seen with office lighting.

> ***"The Tao of Pooh, she read. By Benjamin Hoff."***

This book had been published in the spring of the previous year and given to me as a birthday present by my mother. The author had intended it to be an introduction to the Eastern belief system of Taoism for Westerners. It begins with a description of the vinegar tasters, which is a painting portraying the three great Eastern thinkers, Confucius, the Buddha, and Laozi sitting over a vat of vinegar. Each tasting the vinegar of "life," Confucius finds it sour; the Buddha finds it bitter, but Laozi, the traditional founder of Taoism, finds it satisfying. The story unfolds rhythmically, backing up this analogy.

I told Molly the story of how my mother had checked this book out at the library as soon as it was available. She has always been interested in Eastern religions and philosophy and was curious as to how Winnie the Pooh could be connected. She hoped I would enjoy it and it had quickly become a favorite for me. It was still on The New York Times bestseller's list and many people were becoming interested in Taoism.

It's interesting to note here that twenty-five years later I would meet Benjamin Hoff's nephew, Geoff, and that our lives would become intertwined most magically.

We were at a marketing event in Austin, Texas and he said something about Winnie the Pooh. I then said something about the Tao of Pooh and he matter-of-factly stated that his uncle had written a book with that title. He was a writer and came from a long line of writers on his father's side of the family. His father was a poet of some acclaim who now lived in mainland China. Geoff's dream was to visit him there but he passed away in 2015 before he could make the trip.

Over the next two days, I thought about the strategies Molly had shared with me and was ready to take action. She had said that thinking about anything could only take you so far and I agreed. The solution to my problem was to work actively on making a sale and taking some listings, with the immediate intention of arranging a lease of a rental property in the short run. It turned out that I would be paid almost immediately when a lease was signed and that was exactly what I was interested in at that time.

Our office had rental listings in a white binder that was kept on the top shelf of a locked bookcase next to the restroom. I'm not sure why they would be hidden away like this but Molly did have the key. I poured over them for two hours before choosing a new apartment building less than a mile from our office. I asked Molly why almost all of the units were still vacant if the complex had been completed almost two months ago.

> ***"Location, location, location," she answered with the smile I had now become accustomed to her wearing.***

I drove by the building that afternoon and it was gorgeous. The modern architecture was quite appealing. I parked and walked around to the side and could see landscaping that had been meticulously cared for so that the tenants would have a small park-like setting to enjoy. No one seemed to be there for me to ask so I drove back to the office and put my plan into action.

I called the office of the Recycler, a publication that had listings for everything you could imagine. I placed a small print ad that described the one and two-bedroom apartments that were available for lease. When people called, I told them that I would be showing each of the units on Sunday morning and to come to my office at eight so they could follow me there.

On Sunday morning, at not quite eight o'clock and before the summer sun was high in the sky my people began showing up. There were half a dozen cars and one large truck. When everyone who had called me had arrived, we formed a caravan to drive over to the property. When we arrived, I unlocked the doors of the vacant units one by one and let the people walk through them on their own. At some point, one person asked to see the balcony, and several people followed us as I unlocked the French doors and went outside.

In an instant, I knew why fourteen of the sixteen units were still vacant after more than two months. Although the building was new, the location was highly desirable, and the apartments were spacious and modern, there was one drawback that was glaringly obvious when you stood out on the balconies: This building sat adjacent to the Ventura freeway north on-ramp.

As some of us gathered to see the view a car drove up the on-ramp and paused at the red light that limited how many people could enter the freeway at a time. The man driving turned and waved at us and I waved back. To the astonished people standing behind me and waiting for an explanation I simply turned to them and said,

> *"Welcome to 'On Ramp View Estates,' where convenience and ease of access is our goal."*

I rented eight apartments that day. The man who had come in the commercial truck was a general contractor on a large commercial project close by and needed housing for his workers. A couple signed up when they found out it was alright to have their large dog. An older couple chose a one-bedroom unit on the third floor because they said the combination of location, price, and easy freeway access made it a conversation starter that could not be duplicated. Ten days later I received my commission check for over four thousand dollars. I took Molly out to lunch the following day.

While this story was intended to be entertaining, the truth is that when I discovered I was something of a natural when it came to marketing my life was forever changed.

It hadn't been a coincidence that I was the one figuring out how my mother and could have a roof over our heads, food to eat, and clothes to wear while I was growing up. I always had my next idea for how to bring in some money and this kept us out of the poor house on many occasions.

I am so grateful that my mother lived to see me become a published author of three books and an entrepreneur with an online business. She was ninety-three when she died in 2011. During those last five years of her life, I had the time and the money to do everything I wanted with and for her.

Marketing Yourself and Everything You Do

With marketing as your superpower, you can get the word out about yourself and others. One of the highlights of my year back in 2019 was helping a teenager in my community with his Eagle Scout Project.

It was only by chance that I found out he needed help with this project and that if he didn't keep to his schedule, he would not be able to complete everything in time. The Boy Scouts of America had graciously given him a one-year extension, but time was running out before his 19th birthday, which would forever render him ineligible to accomplish this goal he had held since he was a little boy. This is what I posted on my personal Facebook page:

I have a personal request today. A young man in my community has been going through some challenges with health and depression. This Saturday I will be helping him with his Eagle Scout project and he is short of funds. The family is stretched thin with medical expenses. If you feel so inclined, please donate $5 - no more - to his fund. I want him to know what it's like to have people who don't know you believe in you. Kyle is a wonderful young man with a bright future, once he can make it through this tough time. Thank you in advance.

Kyle had set up his own GoFundMe page and this is the story he shared:

Help the animals at Hart Park in Newhall! I am doing an Eagle Scout Project to install 1,000 ft. of rattlesnake fencing to protect the deer and horse pens at the park animal exhibits. This will cost upwards of 1,400 dollars and my immediate family does not have the money for this and we are on a deadline.

This is an exciting project for me because I did not think that I would be able to complete my Eagle project! I was just about there when I began having health issues due to an undisclosed medical condition and resulting depression. The past two years have been dark, but BSA (Boy Scouts of America) approved a one-year extension for me to complete this even though I aged out almost one year ago on my 18th birthday. Please consider a small donation to help the animals, so we

If this is work you feel called to do, please pick up a copy of my book, "Local Business Marketing: Making the Phone Ring for Businesses Everywhere" wherein I have given you the blueprint for getting started with this rewarding and lucrative business model. People all over the world have learned from me, and my most successful local business marketer to date is a woman helping brick-and-mortar and online businesses in a small city in Australia.

Doing the Work

While anyone can become a marketer, few are willing to do the work to achieve this as a goal. They get very excited, read a book or two, tell a couple of people what they're doing, and then fizzle out fairly quickly. I can recognize this modus operandi a mile away and it is far too common, I believe.

The reason I can so easily recognize when someone is not going to follow through or be consistent for even thirty days is because that described me until I came online in 2006.

I was a complainer who thought everyone else could achieve goals and dreams, while I could not.

You must be willing to do the work. The deep work that will stretch you to your limits, or at least to the limits you've been busy creating for yourself during your lifetime.

In a previous chapter, I shared the quote I have come to be known by, both in my personal life and in my business:

> *"Do for a year what others won't; Live, forever the way others can't."*

The people I mentor in either one of my programs are used to me asking them if they've begun their year yet. I am gentle but firm when I tell them they must take action every single day to maintain consistency. If you stop for thirty days or more, you are almost back at the beginning when you commence your activities again.

I encourage you to start your year right this second and move forward with zest and gusto!

EPILOGUE

By the waters, the waters of Babylon
We lay down and wept, and wept, for thee Zion
We remember thee, remember thee, remember thee, Zion.

~ By the Waters of Babylon, adapted from Psalm 137 by Jeremiah and covered by various artists over the years

We can have anything we want in life, as long as we know what it is that we are striving towards and are willing to go after it with dedication, inspiration, and in the spirit of serving others.

My life changed dramatically and significantly during my first year online, even though I didn't yet know exactly what I wanted in my life. Everything was moving quickly, but instead of deciding that I would maintain this new position and be satisfied with what I had achieved, I chose to stay on the ride and hang on for as long as possible to discover what could come next. I'm still on this journey and thank God every day for His tender mercies.

I'll share a few of the concepts I've learned about, and please know that I realize much of this sounds like science fiction. Having access to a hand-held computer that would be available to people all over the planet sounded far-fetched when I was in college; smartphones are now available in even the most remote corners of the world, and services like Starlink ensure they are connected to the Internet. Keep an open mind.

I learned about terraforming by reading a short story titled "Collision Orbit" which was originally written in 1942. The author was Jack Williamson, using the pseudonym "Will Stewart."

Terraforming is the hypothetical process of deliberately modifying the atmosphere, temperature, surface topography, or ecology of a planet, moon, or other body to be similar to the environment of Earth to make it habitable for humans to live on. The concept of terraforming developed from both science fiction and actual science. Astronomer Carl Sagan proposed the planetary engineering of Venus in 1961, which is considered one of the first accounts of the concept. My belief is that what is happening on our planet and in our galaxy is terraforming in reverse.

The science will tell us that what I'm sharing here is not possible, but I believe there is more to the story than initially meets the eye. I have had personal experiences where I made a lateral arabesque into a parallel universe that opened me up to receiving miracles in my life that have no logical explanation. Someday, people may think it odd that we didn't adapt the atmosphere of Mars and Venus to the Earth.

Perhaps these are experiences that haven't yet occurred, or ones that need to affect people in ways we aren't yet ready to explore. I will encourage you to 'Google' this topic of terraforming if it's of interest to you. And consider the writings of R. Buckminster Fuller and his work in synergetics to have a more complete picture of what I am describing here.

What will your future bring? By now you know it's completely up to you, with a few exceptions to allow for mindset shifts. Having the ability to earn an excellent income from home, or from wherever in the world you happen to be is a gift not to be taken lightly. An internet connection is now an expectation for most of us, and we're moving closer every day to it being taken for granted by everyone.

> *"The ship sang of the beauty of Order, of perfect symmetry and ultimate peace. It glided through the calm blackness of space, absorbing it. Energy circulated through its petals in a regular rhythm. The serenity of its silent passage, the unity of its functioning. The satisfaction of service wove through its melody.*
> *Ahead, a blue-and-white orb glowed in the blackness, the goal of the journey. The ship slipped through the stillness toward it, following Kosh's direction eagerly. Obedience was its greatest joy."*

~ J. Michael Straczynski, Babylon 5

can protect them from the increase in snake bites the park is experiencing!

The donations began to come in almost immediately, and several hundred people connected to me on social media and also on my email list were excited to help Kyle reach his goal.

I called his mother several hours later and asked her to look at his GoFundMe page. She went silent when she saw that he was getting to his goal quickly, then thanked me through her tears in a soft voice.

By midnight that night, Kyle had raised twice as much as he needed and called me to thank me and to ask me to tell everyone they didn't need to donate any more money. I suggested we wait until morning and then tell everyone that he was going to donate all of the additional money to another Boy Scout in a similar situation. He liked that idea very much.

I was one of the volunteers at the park on Saturday. When we took a lunch break, Kyle and I had the chance to speak away from the others. Before me stood a young man who was now taller than he ever thought he could be, but just as tall as I always knew he could be. I don't recall our conversation exactly on that day, but now he is a happy young man in his twenties who plans to get married next year. And by the way, Kyle is currently working for a technology company in Silicon Valley, and his specialties are marketing and copywriting.

Marketing for Others as a Business Model

I was recently a featured speaker and presenter at an event for non-profits, local businesses, and school districts in California. They asked me to speak because of my vast experience in all aspects of marketing, but also because of the book I wrote several years ago titled "Local Business Marketing: Making the Phone Ring for Businesses Everywhere" which became an overnight bestseller when it was initially released.

Earlier in this book I shared that I had begun my marketing journey by helping a family member with his new handyman business.

ABOUT THE AUTHOR

"Be creative, imagine the life you want to live, and then take massive action to move closer to your goals. You can do it, and I believe in you."

~ Connie Ragen Green

Connie Ragen Green is a bestselling author, international speaker, and online marketing strategist who is dedicating her life to serving others as they build and grow successful and lucrative online businesses.

Her background includes working as a classroom teacher for twenty years in the inner city of Los Angeles, while simultaneously working in real estate as a listing broker and residential appraiser. At the end of the school year in 2006 she left it all behind to come online, and the rest is history.

She makes her home in two cities in southern California; Santa Clarita in the desert and Santa Barbara at the beach. In addition to her writing and work online, Connie consults and strategizes with several major corporations and some non-profits, as well as volunteering with groups such as the international service organization Rotary, the Boys & Girls Clubs, the women's business organization Zonta, and several other charitable groups.

As the recent recipient of the Merrill Hoffman Award, presented to Connie by the Santa Barbara Rotary Club, being honored with this award has strengthened her resolve to serve others around the world in any way she is able to by using her gifts, talents, and experiences positively and sincerely. Her online business is the vehicle for this and Connie continues to serve new and seasoned entrepreneurs, authors, and speakers.

View all of Connie's books at http://ConnieRagenGreenBooks.com and discover more about her at https://Linktr.ee/ConnieRagenGreen

Made in the USA
Monee, IL
04 November 2026

67380148R00128